CASTLE HOTELS
IN
AUSTRIA

PAUL V. JAMESON
HANNAH JAMESON

Printed by Cummings Printing Company
P.O. Box 16495
Hooksett, NH 03106-6495

ISBN 0-9649052-0-5

For information address questions to:
EURAMCO
15 Elm Street
Canton, MA 02021

Manufactured in the United States of America

ACKNOWLEDGEMENTS

We wish to express thanks to all members of our family for their encouragement and unselfish support in this project, and especially to Betty Jameson, our wife and mother, whose many suggestions have enriched the end result.

We are deeply indebted to Mrs. Irene Donoghue for turning an illegible manuscript into a readable one, and to Miss Pollyanna Andem for the long hours she spent in editing it.

Our thanks go to hotel managers who kindly gave us some of the photographs, and special thanks to Miss Gabriele Wolf from the Austrian National Tourist Office in New York for providing volumes of information on Austrian castles and for her generous help all along the way.

CONTENTS

FOREWORD

Castles bring to mind half-forgotten tales about the enchanted world of yore, about emperors and kings, valiant knights, handsome princes and beautiful princesses, who lived in slender castles in the midst of forests inhabited by stately stags, gentle deer, and graceful swans. This magical world of childhood fantasies for which even grown people secretly long seems almost real in Austria, where forests still abound in wildlife and hundreds of well-preserved castles even now dot the countryside. Many of them continue to be the exclusive preserve of descendants of their original owners, but quite a few welcome guests.

Austria is renowned for the great beauty of its landscape and for its glorious cities that overflow with priceless cultural treasures, but her true treasure and her greatest asset are the happy and outgoing country people, who on Sundays and festive occasions still dress in regional costumes, not as a show for tourists, but spontaneously, in reverence of their roots and traditions. As most castle hotels are outside cities, they provide an opportunity to get to know these friendly common people and to see the natural beauty of the country while enjoying the comfort and charm of an old castle. Surprisingly, prices at castle hotels are not higher than at other hotels of comparable category; therefore, all the magic they provide comes free.

Whatever else you may do in Austria, do not spend your vacation racing from city to city. Slow down, get out of the car, and walk or rest in the majestic countryside, for nature in Austria is said to recompense richly all who linger in it long enough to reap her rewards. Relax and unwind, and at least while there, let yourself be guided by the maxim:

Das Leben froh genießen
Ist der Vernunft Gebot,
Man lebt ja nur so kurze Zeit
Und ist so lange tot.

(Common sense demands that we enjoy life, for we live only a short time and are dead so long.)

If you find this book helpful in planning your trip to Austria, it will have accomplished its objective; but if it also helps you to find the castle of your childhood dreams, it will have fulfilled our fondest hopes.

1

INTRODUCTION

This travel guide is intended primarily for prospective visitors to Austria who have the interest and the time to plan their own vacation, but it may also be helpful to travel agents, who advise individuals or small groups on where to go, what to see and what to do once they arrive there. As its title indicates, it concerns itself primarily with the charm and the magic of castle hotels.

The book first provides general information on the country and its people and then offers specific information on each of Austria's nine provinces and forty of its castle hotels. Several other castle hotels found lacking in comfort or in ambiance have been left out, and the ones listed here have at least a three-star rating.

In many instances description of hotels is followed by suggestions for excursions, but the enjoyable walks, hikes, and sightseeing tours are too numerous to describe them all. Receptionists at hotels will gladly tell you about them and will often also provide detailed trail maps and sightseeing brochures.

The prices quoted here are valid for the year 1995, but as they change every year and vary from one season to another, we urge you to have your travel agent give you a price update at the time of booking.

GEOGRAPHY

Austria used to be the center of a vast empire but is now only a relatively small, land-locked country covering an area of 83,855 sq. km (square kilometers). Located in Central Europe, Austria is bordered by Germany to the north and northwest, the Czech Republic to the north and northeast, Slovakia and Hungary to the east, Slovenia and Italy to the south, and Switzerland and Liechtenstein to the west. The country is about 550 km long, and has a maximum width of 280 km.

The topography of Austria is dominated by the Alps, which cover about 2/3 of the country, including the western, central, and southern regions. The highest peak is the Großglockner (3,797 m) in the Hohe Tauern mountains, but there are many other peaks high enough to be covered all year by a thick blanket of snow and ice. The remaining 1/3 of the country is occupied by the heavily wooded foothills of the Alps, which extend to the valley of the Danube, the Vienna basin, and the Hungarian Plain.

The largest river is the Danube, whose source is found in the park behind Prince Fürstenberg's palace in Donaueschingen, in the Black Forest region of Germany. From here, the Danube flows for 2,900 km through Germany, Austria, Slovakia, Hungary, Yugoslavia, Romania, and Bulgaria into the Black Sea. It is the second largest river in Europe and the only major river flowing from west to east. Unfortunately, the Danube is also the route taken by many armies. Charlemagne's armies and the crusaders traveled down the Danube from west to east, while Huns, Hungarians, and Turks pressed their attacks in the opposite direction. But in peace, commerce flowed in both directions bringing prosperity to all.

Bodensee at the western end of the country is the largest lake in Europe and is shared by Germany, Switzerland, and Austria. The second largest lake in the country is the Neusiedlersee on the border between Austria and Hungary.

Austria has about 7.6 million inhabitants of whom about 1.6 million live in Vienna. The second largest city is Graz with 245,000 inhabitants, followed by Linz with 200,000, Salzburg with 140,000, and Innsbruck with 117,000. The country consists of nine *Länder* (provinces), which from west to east are Vorarlberg, Tirol, Salzburg, Kärnten (Carinthia), Steiermark (Styria), Oberösterreich (Upper Austria), Niederösterreich (Lower Austria), Burgenland, and Wien (Vienna).

The climate is subalpine, neither too hot nor too cold, but is greatly influenced by the local topography. There is snow in the valleys between December and March, and in the mountains between November and the end of April. Permanent snow is found in elevations of over 2,500 m and also in considerably lower lying ravines deep enough to shield the snow from the sun.

A peculiarity of the Austrian climate is the Föhn, a very strong and warm wind from the Mediterranean, which blows in early spring or fall and causes fatigue, headache, irritability, and numerous other complaints.

The most favorable months for hiking in the Alps are June, September, and early October, when the weather is comfortably warm, relatively dry, and sunny.

In Vienna the weather is best in spring and autumn, while the height of the season in the lake areas is in July and August. Skiing is best between late December and April, but there are several easily accessible glaciers where one can ski all year.

Austria's economy is fairly well diversified and the country is endowed with a very well-educated work force, ample hydroelectric power, excellent roads, strong manufacturing industry, and thriving agriculture. Austria abounds with natural beauty and has done more than most other countries to protect and preserve it. The natural beauty of the country and its cultural treasures attract a large number of foreign tourists, about 18 million in 1993. Most came from Germany but about 680,000 came from the UK, 540,000 from the US, and 75,000 from Canada. In the same year, the annual per capita income from tourism was 22,000 ATS, higher than in any other country. The tourist industry provides about 500,000 jobs and accounts for 25% of all Austrian exports.

HISTORY

The population of Austria is predominantly of Germanic extraction. Its western part was settled by the Alemanns, the tribe that also settled much of Switzerland, while the rest of the country was settled by the Baiuvarii (Bavarians). In 996 the country was for the first time referred to as Osterrichi - the eastern state - as it was the easternmost German-speaking land. This name evolved into its present name - Österreich. In 1156 it became a hereditary duchy under the rule of the Babenberg dynasty, that made Vienna their capital. They left a rich legacy of monasteries and churches, promoted literacy, and it was during their reign that an anonymous author recorded the old saga of the Nibelungs. Following the death of the last Babenberg in a battle with the Hungarians, Rudolph von Habsburg, a previously little known count from northern Switzerland, was elected to the throne in 1273, and his descendants reigned until 1918. The Habsburgs gradually expanded their domain more through strategic marriages than through wars. As emperors of the Holy Roman Empire founded by Charlemagne in the year 800, they at one time or other ruled over Austria, Germany, Hungary, Belgium, the Netherlands, the Czech lands, Slovakia, Slovenia, Croatia, and Bosnia, parts of France, Switzerland, Poland, Ukraine, Romania, and Serbia, as well as over Spain and its vast overseas empire. At the zenith of their might in the 16th century, theirs was the first ever empire over which the sun truly never set. In the 17th century, parts of Austria were devastated in the Thirty Years' War between the Catholic and Protestant countries of Europe, during which the Protestant Swedish army at one point reached the outskirts of Vienna. Even more suffering was caused by Turkish invasions in the 16th and the 17th centuries.. In the second Turkish invasion in 1683, Vienna was besieged and was barely saved by the joined forces of Austria, the German principalities, and Poland. Prince Eugene of Savoy, the most famous Austrian military leader, won final victory over the Turks in 1697 and thus put an end to Turkish incursions into Central Europe.

The dominant figure of the 18th century history of Austria was Empress Maria Theresia, who reigned for 40 years (1740-1780). She was succeeded by Joseph II, "The Enlightened Despot." During their reigns public schooling was improved, freedom of religion was introduced, torture was prohibited, and serfdom was abolished. In the early part of the 19th century, Austria was repeatedly invaded by Napoleon's army,

7

which brutally suppressed the revolt of the brave Tirolean peasants and executed their leader, Andreas Hofer. He was, and still is, the pride of Tirol, as revered by Austrians as Wilhelm Tell is by the Swiss. In 1806, when the Austrian emperor was forced by Napoleon to relinquish the old and prestigeous but by then purely ceremonial title of Emperor of the Holy Roman Empire, he assumed the newly created title of Emperor of Austria. Toward the end of the Napoleonic Wars, in 1813, Prince Schwarzenberg (see: Hotel im Palais Schwarzenberg, Vienna) was in command of all the allied forces in the decisive battle of Leipzig, in which Napoleon was routed. The battle plan was actually drawn by Schwarzenberg's young chief of staff, Count Radetzky, whose name was later immortalized by Johann Strauss the Elder in his famous *Radetzky Marsch*.

Of all the Habsburg emperors, none is remembered with more fondness than Franz Josef, who reigned for 68 years from 1848 to 1916. He left a lasting imprint on the country most evident in Vienna, where his portraits are still prominently displayed in restaurants and coffee houses. He is remembered as a benevolent and unpretentious emperor who lived a Spartan life and slept in a standard military bed in a small, sparsely furnished room without running water or electricity. Despite the tragedies that destroyed his family life - his beautiful wife was stabbed to death by an Italian anarchist in Switzerland, and his only son committed suicide - - he unswervingly discharged his onerous duties to the very end. During his reign the whole country prospered, Vienna grew rapidly, most of its present landmark buildings were erected, and the city became the musical capital of the world. The long simmering discord caused by the Hungarians' demands for independence was resolved amicably. Two years after his death and immediately after World War I, the Habsburgs were deposed, Hungary and all the Slav lands of the Empire split off from Austria, and the small remaining Austria was forced to cede the southern part of Tirol to Italy.

Austria has since been a federal republic. On January 1, 1995, it joined the European Union.

The present pretender to its throne, Archduke Otto von Habsburg, lives in exile in the neighboring German state of Bavaria from which he was elected to the European Parliament in Strasbourg.

CULTURE

Language

The language of Austria is German, but its pronunciation is slightly different from that in Germany and Switzerland and also varies from one province to another. A visitor to Austria who learned German by using textbooks or language tapes from Germany will be surprised to hear Austrians greet him with *Grüß Gott* and *Aufwiederschauen* instead of the expected *Guten Tag* and *Aufwiedersehen*. Potatoes are called *Erdäpfel*, not *Kartoffeln*, while tomatoes are *Paradeiser*, not *Tomaten*, and cream in your coffee is *Obers*, not *Sahne*. Everybody, of course, understands the standard German but will feel greatly flattered if you use the local expression.

In face to face conversation, English speaking people rarely have much difficulty in understanding the essence of what a reasonably well-educated German-speaking person is trying to say, but may have difficulty with the written German. Letters of the two alphabets are identical except for the German letter *ß* used in *Schloß* (castle) and *Straße* (road). This is pronounced like **SS** in English. The German *v* sounds like **F**, and *w* like **V**. The German *a* is pronounced **AH**, and the *e* like the English **A**. The *i* is pronounced like **E**, while *u* sounds like **OO** in the word boot. The *Umlaut* (two dots above vowels *ä*, *ö*, *ü*) slightly changes their pronunciation, but you will be understood even if you pronounce these vowels as if the little dots were absent. The diphthong *ie* is pronounced like the English **EE**, *ei* like **I**, and *eu* like **OY** in the word oyster. Finally, if a word begins with an *s* followed by *t* or *p*, it is pronounced like the English **SH**.

If all this sounds confusing, take heart: all young people in Austria understand and even speak some English, which is taught in school, while virtually all people in the tourist trade have at least a working knowledge of the English language and are eager to practice it.

Music

Austria has a strong musical tradition and was for many years home to the leading composers. Mozart composed over 600 works still played in concert halls all over the world. Haydn, the greatest master of the symphonic form, was the author of more than 100 symphonies. A majestic tune from one of his compositions became the Austrian imperial anthem.. Later on, Germany adopted the same tune for its national

9

anthem but completely changed its words. Beethoven, who was born in Germany but lived in Austria, composed beautiful sonatas and piano and violin concertos but is especially famous for his symphonies. Tragically, he began losing his hearing at the age of 28 and composed his magnificent 9th symphony when he had already been completely deaf for four years. The stirring *Ode to Joy* from this masterpiece of his is now the national anthem of the European Union. Schubert, the Hungarian born Liszt, Brahms, Bruckner,and Mahler followed in the steps of these giants.

In the second half of the nineteenth century, Vienna became entranced by the waltz, an Austrian folk dance, which through the Strauss family's numerous light and happy compositions soon captivated all Europe. It is said that Johann Strauss the Younger alone composed more than 400 of them. The other hallmark of the musical scene of late 19th century Vienna was the operetta, of which *Die Fledermaus* by J. Strauss the Younger is the most popular. It is still part of the permanent repertoire of both Vienna's Opera Companies. Other highly regarded composers of operettas were the Hungarian born Franz Lehár, especially applauded for *Die Lustige Witwe* (The Merry Widow) and Kálmán, who introduced a strong Hungarian flavor to this musical genre.

No account of Austrian music is complete without touching on folk music, which best reflects the cheerfulness of the people of this country. Yodeling and the physically demanding *Schuhplattler* dancing are perfect expressions of their youthful energy and ebullience. These forms of art have reached the highest level of perfection in the Tirol, where there are almost daily *Tirolerabend* performances in major tourist centers. Instead of attending one of these technically perfect but somewhat staged spectacles in large and crowded halls, you could go to one of the less proficiently executed but more genuine productions in village inns, where local amateur performers are cheered on by a high-spirited audience of relatives and neighbors. Very enjoyable also are their quaint Sunday parades and concerts. Immediately after church, villagers dressed in regional costumes proudly march to the center of the village, where their brass band then enthusiastically plays oompah music to the delight of all.

Architecture

A striking feature of the landscape of solidly Roman Catholic Austria are the numerous churches and chapels dotting the countryside and gracing the hilltops, as is also the large crosses (*Gipfelkreuz*) visible from afar that mark the summits of mountains. Religion has been an integral part of Austrian culture and has through the centuries inspired not only their composers and artists but has also motivated their emperors and nobles to build churches and monasteries. In the 12th century they were built in the Romanesque style and beginning in the late 13th century, in the Gothic style. After the religious strife and the second Turkish invasion in the 17th century, there was a surge of construction in the Baroque style. Unfortunately, excessive enthusiasm for this new style caused many old Romanesque and Gothic churches to be modified to conform to the taste of the period; thus, only a few purely Romanesque or purely Gothic monuments now remain. The Baroque was undoubtedly Austria's most brilliant architectural period. Its most prominent representatives were Fischer von Erlach the Elder and the Younger, and Lucas von Hildebrandt. In its later stages, the Baroque style evolved into the exceedingly ornate Rococo before changing into the more restrained Neoclassical style. Visitors to Austria will notice that an unusually large number of buildings are painted ocher yellow, a color rarely seen elsewhere. This particular shade of yellow happened to be Maria Theresia's favorite color. She chose it for the exterior of the Schönbrunn Palace from where its popularity spread to smaller palaces in the provinces, to churches, public buildings, and even military barracks. It remains a favorite throughout the country.

Between 1857 and 1891, the face of Vienna changed dramatically. The huge fortified wall around the Inner City was replaced by a vast new boulevard lined with imposing government buildings, museums, and theaters, all built in the same grand style that to this day remains the dominant architectural style of the capital.

Etiquette

The rules of behavior of polite people reflect the values of that society and as such are an integral part of that society's culture. Austrians in general are courteous and considerate. They treat old people with respect and as their society is less egalitarian than most, they show deference to those whom they perceive as their superiors. They are fascinated by titles and use them even when the person in question has only the remotest possible claim to it. Physicians, PhD's and all lawyers are routinely addressed with *Herr* or *Frau Doktor*, and even wives of the assorted *Herr Doktors* are often extended the courtesy title of *Frau Doktor*. The title of *Herr* or *Frau Professor* is generously accorded to

11

many teachers, while graduates of engineering schools are called *Herr Ingeneur*. Special deference is shown to members of the nobility indicated by the *von* (pronounced: fon) before the family name. Even here distinction is made between a simple *von*, who is of lower rank than a *Graf* (count), who in turn is no match to a *Fürst* (prince) or an *Erzherzog* (archduke).

Handshaking is much more common than in the English speaking countries and is accompanied by a nod or a slight bow. Ladies are addressed with *Gnädige Frau* (merciful lady) and are greeted with *Küss die Hand* (I kiss your hand). A very polite gentleman actually kisses the lady's proffered hand. It is customary in Austria to send flowers to the hostess before arriving for a visit. When ordering flowers, you should tell the florist for what occasion they are intended and ask for guidance, because the choice of flowers, their color, and even their number have implications of which you are most likely unaware.

Strict adherence to these rules of etiquette is expected from a polite Austrian but not necessarily from a foreigner. All that is really expected from you is civility, but any additional courtesy will be noted, acknowledged,and will be greatly appreciated.

FOOD

Food could very appropriately have been discussed in the chapter on Austrian culture as it is an integral part of it. We are devoting a separate chapter to this "table culture" only because the topic is vast and is of great practical interest to visitors. The *Wiener Küche* (Viennese cooking) blends the Bavarian cuisine with influences from Hungary and Slav parts of the former Austro-Hungarian Empire. The food is flavorful but rather rich. The main meal of the day is lunch but in addition to the three meals a day that we are used to, there is the *Jause*. It is a midafternoon meal when open-faced sandwiches are served or, more likely, pastries accompanied by tea, coffee, or hot chocolate usually with whipped cream (*Schlagobers*, or simply *Schlag*). The price of food in restaurants is reasonable, especially that of fixed-price meals called *Menü*, which generally cost 25-30% less than the same courses ordered à la carte. Food in taverns and country inns is excellent and is always cheaper than in restaurants. The least expensive meals are found at food stalls selling *Wurst* (sausage) with *Senf* (mustard) or *Kren* (horse radish).

Soups
Soups are eaten at lunch and also often at dinnertime. The most popular are the very tasteful *Leberknödlsuppe*, made of broth and chicken liver dumplings, and the *Gulaschsuppe*, an originally Hungarian soup made of small cubes of beef and a lot of sweet paprika.

Meats
The most famous Austrian meat dish is the *Wiener Schnitzel*, a breaded veal cutlet fried to a golden brown color, but the meat dish Austrians prefer to all others is *Rindfleisch* (boiled beef). The best kind of boiled beef is the *Tafelspitz*, served in most Austrian homes on Sundays and festive occasions. *Reh* and *Hirsch* (kinds of deer), *Gams* (mountain goat), and *Wildschwein* (wild boar) taste delicious and are fitting choices for dinners at castle hotels. The tender and juicy *Backhendl* (fried chicken) also should not be missed.

Fish

The imported salt-water fish dishes look and taste as they do in every other country, but fresh *Forelle* (trout) is always delicious as is also fillet of *Zander*, a pike-perch.

Vegetables

The most popular vegetable is potatoes, the most tasteful of which is the *Heurige Erdäpfel* (small young potatoes). Boiled potatoes cooked with butter and sprinkled with parsley are excellent and usually accompany fish dishes.

Austrians are also fond of cabbage. *Sauercraut* is often eaten with pork and *Rotkraut* (red cabbage) with venison.

Bread

Instead of the sliced up, dry, sponge-like supermarket bread we are used to, Austrian bread is fresh and at breakfast often still warm. Its crust is crisp and the middle moist. The same is true of the *Semmel* (roll) and *Kipfel* (crescent) usually served with breakfast.

Desserts

Austrians undoubtedly are world leaders in this branch of the culinary art. Every housewife makes outstanding *Strudel* of thin sheets of dough, rolled up and filled with apples, cherries, or cheese, and then baked. They all make *Kaiserschmarrn*, a uniquely Austrian dessert made of crumbled pancakes and served with preserves. It derives its name from an event in the 19th century when the emperor was forced to take shelter in a hut where he was offered *Schmarrn,* a simple peasant dish he had never tasted. The cold and hungry emperor declared the lowly *Schmarrn* food fit for an emperor and renamed it *Kaiserschmarrn.* Other common desserts are *Marillenknödel* and *Zwetschgenknödel*, dumplings filled with apricots or plums; *Buchteln,* jam-filled yeast dumplings; and *Guglhupf,* a ring-shaped, ribbed cake especially tasty when made with chocolate. The easy to prepare *Palatschinken,* thin, rolled up pancakes stuffed with jam, chocolate, or cheese, are of Hungarian origin but are now standard fare in Austrian homes and restaurants. Somewhat more sophisticated is *Salzburger Nockerln,* a fluffy soufflé, but the most highly regarded dessert is the *Torte* (layered cake) of which the *Sachertorte* is the best known. It is a chocolate cake which tastes particularly good when served with *Schlag* (whipped cream) and is said to be best at the

Hotel Sacher in Vienna. Our favorite, however, is the *Dobostorte*, a chocolate layered cake topped by a layer of crisp caramel.

Beverages

Water, unless marked: *Kein Trinkwasser*, is excellent everywhere in the country, and Vienna is said to have purer and better tasting water than any other European capital. It is, therefore, surprising that water is not offered with any meals except with coffee in coffee houses. When one asks for water, *Mineralwasser* (mineral water) is brought. If you insist on having *Normales Wasser* (plain water) you will, of course, get it, but the waiter will clearly begin to wonder about your taste and your solvency.

Beer is good and inexpensive. Local beers are generally preferred but an excellent imported beer is the Czech *Pilsner*.

There is a long wine making tradition in Austria. There are now about 25,000 acres of vineyards mostly in lower Austria and particularly in the Wachau area on the left bank of the Danube, near Vienna. As with beer, it is best to order a local wine. Chances are it will be good, and if ordered in a carafe, also inexpensive.

LODGING

A castle hotel is a castle turned into a hotel in which the ambiance of a castle survives. This definition is not precise as ambiance cannot be measured by objective criteria but is subjectively assessed. Even the word castle is not very specific as it includes five distinct categories of buildings:

- *Burg* is a strategically located medieval building, a fortress-like home of a nobleman, symbol of his independence and proof of his might.
- *Schloß* is a nobleman's residence from more recent times. It served no military purpose but was built for comfort and social status.
- *Palais* (palace) is a particularly opulent *Schloß* usually built for an emperor, king, or prince.
- *Jagdschloß* is the hunting lodge of an aristocrat. It is always smaller, cozier, and more rustic than a *Schloß*.
- *Herrenhaus* is a manor house on a country estate and is considerably less elegant than a *Schloß*.

Most castle hotels give the impression of serene prosperity, but at some, alas, slightly frayed rugs or neglected grounds sadly point to reduced circumstances. All castle hotels have contemporary facilities and provide excellent personalized service that makes one feel not only welcomed but also highly esteemed. Some have indoor swimming pools, Jacuzzis, and saunas, but most offer only outdoor pools and swimming in lakes. Tennis, golf, riding, hunting, fishing, bicycling, walking, and hiking are also available. Buffet breakfast is almost always included in the price of the room. It consists of coffee, tea or hot chocolate, milk, cream, yogurt, cereals, several kinds of bread, rolls, honey, jams, eggs, ham, sausages, cold cuts, cheeses, juices, fresh fruit, and stewed prunes or figs. After a meal as copious as this, one is unlikely to work up an appetite before dinner. Therefore, it makes little sense to sign up for full board when half board is all that is needed.

Unless indicated otherwise, the hotel prices quoted here are prices of double rooms valid for the year 1995.

Advance booking is always desirable but is essential during the main season. When planning your itinerary, you should consider leaving a few days between scheduled stays at castle hotels to spend them in country inns. A good way to find one is to check the map of the area, choose a remote valley, and drive in it to the end of the road, where you will always find a pretty, rustic, inexpensive, and immaculately clean inn more than adequate for a short stay. This interlude will make you appreciate even more the comfort and relative luxury of your next castle hotel.

TRAVEL

Planning of a vacation should begin several months in advance by reading about Austria and the areas of the country you intend to visit. We highly recommend the book *Austria* from the *Insight Guides* series by APA Publications, *The Visitor's Guide to Austria* by Ken Allan, a publication of Hunter Publishing, Inc., and Baedeker's *Austria*. Useful information can also be found in many other standard travel guides. The nearest Austrian National Tourist Office is an excellent source of valuable information, catalogs, and brochures. Be sure to purchase a map of the whole country such as the Rand McNally-Hallwag or the Kümmerley + Frey, available at most major book stores. You will also need more detailed maps of the areas of particular interest, and we recommend *Die General Karte* series by Mairs Verlag, where 1 cm on the map equals a distance of 2 km and where scenic roads, castles, and other points of special interest are marked. These maps can be ordered in the U.S. by calling 1-800-521-6722 or by writing to *Gemütlichkeit*, 2892 Chronicle Avenue, Hayward, CA 94542.

By Air

Vienna's Schwechat airport, 16-17 km east of the city, is served by about 30 international airlines and from it there are connecting flights to Graz, Linz, Salzburg, Innsbruck, and Klagenfurt. The most favorable discount rate for transatlantic flights is the APEX which applies only to tickets purchased at least three weeks before departure, and only for stays in Europe of between 7 and 90 days. These tickets are non cancelable. As Vienna is a considerable distance from the scenic areas of western and central Austria including Tirol, visitors to these areas often fly to Zurich, Frankfurt, or Munich, from where they take connecting flights to the appropriate regional airports in Austria or continue to Austria by road.

By Road

Many visitors from overseas enter Austria by road in cars rented at the Zurich or Munich airports. Your travel agent will obtain brochures for you from the various car rental companies, and you should not limit your choice only to Hertz and Avis. We have found Auto Europe of 27 Pearl Street, PO Box 7006, Portland, ME 04112, Telephone: 1-800-223-5555, excellent and inexpensive.

It is widely believed that if a car rental is charged to any Gold credit card, the car is automatically so well insured that additional insurance is superfluous. This, unfortunately, is not so as the fine print in credit card agreements clearly states that loss of personal belongings, personal liability and injury to anyone or anything inside or outside the rented car is not covered. As injury to you or others and damage to someone else's property may result in enormous liability, discuss the need for additional insurance with a trusted insurance broker well before your departure. If you plan to stay in Austria 21 days or longer, it will be cheaper to lease a car than to rent one, and Auto Europe offers this option. If at all possible, plan to rent and return the car in the same country to avoid a drop off charge. A value added tax (VAT) is added to the bill in all European countries but is much lower in Switzerland than in Austria or Germany. This is one more reason to fly to Zurich airport rent, a car there, and continue to Austria by road. The border is less than one and one half hours away.

Roads in Austria are very good. The speed limit on autobahns is 130 km/hour; on open roads, 100 km/hour; and elsewhere, 50 km/hour unless otherwise posted. The use of seat belts is mandatory, and no children under the age of 12 are allowed in the front seats. Buses and trams always have right of way. Cars must stop behind trams loading or unloading passengers. There is no passing on the right, and right turns on red are not permitted. In intersections without traffic lights or signs indicating priority, the vehicle on the right has priority. Every car must be equipped with a triangular brakedown sign and a first-aid kit. The maximum permissible blood alcohol level is only 0.8 ml/liter, less than in most other countries. Two beers will put you over this limit and the penalty is high.

If you understand German, tune the car radio to station Ö3 for traffic information given hourly, immediately after the news. The Ö3 wave length is displayed on blue boards along major roads. If you are tuned to it, emergency reports will cut into the regular radio program and, surprisingly, will also cut into the music from the tape in your cassette player. Parking is restricted in most towns, and zones in which parking is restricted are marked by a blue line along the curb. Before parking there, you must obtain a small cardboard clock, which you set on arrival and display on the dashboard for the police to know whether the time limit has been exceeded. In other cities parking vouchers must be used. One can buy them at banks, gas stations, and tobacco shops. Again, mark the time of arrival and display the voucher on the dashboard. If you plan to spend several days in a city, consider turning in your car. You will see more by walking or by using the outstanding and inexpensive public transportation.

By Rail

Austria has an extensive and almost completely electrified rail system which provides punctual and inexpensive transportation. Children under the age of 6 travel free if they do not occupy a separate seat. If they do, they are charged half price as are all children between the ages of 6 and 15. Seniors (women 60 and over and men 65 and over) are entitled to a 50% discount if they have a *Seniorenpass*. This can be obtained by writing to ÖBB-Verkehrseinnahmen Und Reklamationsstelle, A-1090 Wien, Mariannengasse 20, Austria. A photostat of the page in your passport with your photograph and date of birth must be enclosed, as well as a second passport photograph and a traveler's check for $25. A senior citizen's card can also be obtained at railroad stations in Austria during your visit, but it will not benefit you immediately as a period of time must be allowed for processing of the application. The card can be obtained at the main railroad stations in Frankfurt, Munich, and Zurich, and even at the airport railroad station in Zurich.

MONEY MATTERS

Banks

The currency of Austria is the Austrian Schilling (ATS), which is pegged to the German mark at a ratio of 7 schillings to 1 Deutsche Mark, and this ratio is rigidly maintained by the Austrian Central Bank. Its exchange rate to the US dollar and other currencies varies but has lately been about 10 ATS to the dollar. Each Schilling has 100 Groschen. There are coins for 5, 10 and 50 Groschen and for 1, 5 and 10 Schillings. Bank notes come in denominations of 20, 50, 100, 500, 1,000 and 5,000 Schillings.

Bank hours are 8:00 a.m. to 3:00 p.m. except on Thursdays, when banks remain open till 5:30 p.m.. Banks in small towns are closed between 12:30 and 1:30 p.m.. There is no banking on Saturdays, Sundays, and holidays.

Foreign currency is best changed at banks because the exchange rate there is always more favorable than at a *Wechselstube* (money exchange bureau) of which there are many in cities, at bus and railroad stations, and at border crossings. The worst exchange rates are offered by stores, restaurants, and hotels. Never buy more than the bare minimum of Austrian money before entering Austria because the rate of exchange is always best in the country whose currency you are buying. The best rate of all is reserved for international banks and credit card companies that change huge amounts of money every day. You can take advantage of this rate by charging your expenses to a credit card. The amount charged is then converted into your home currency at the best possible rate of the day.

The risk of carrying cash can be avoided by buying traveler's checks. American Express and most banks charge a 1% commission for this, but traveler's checks can now be bought at the AAA (American Automobile Association) and some travel agencies free of commission.

Credit Cards

The most widely accepted credit card is the American Express Card. Its greatest advantage over bank credit cards is that it does not limit your credit. With it, you do not have to worry about currency fluctuations which may suddenly bring your Schilling-denominated charges above your dollar-denominated credit card limit. American Express Gold Cards can be used to obtain cash from a dispenser at the

Vienna airport and from American Express offices in all major cities. The limit on cash advances is the equivalent of $2,500 in Austrian money in any seven day period. The cost of transactions through a dispenser is the greater of 2.5 dollars or 2% of the total amount, but not more than $20 for a single transaction. MasterCard, Visa, and Diners Club cards are also widely accepted, and Visa and MasterCard Gold cards can be used at participating banks to obtain cash up to the credit limit of the card. MasterCard is accepted at most banks, but Bank Austria, the largest in the country, will advance cash to Visa Gold Card holders.

Shopping

Most shops are open on weekdays from 8:30 a.m. or 9:00 a.m. to 6:00 p.m. with a lunch break between noon and 2:00 p.m., or 3:00 p.m. in some villages. Stores in large cities do not close for lunch. On Saturdays, stores close at 1:00 p.m. except on the first Saturday in the month, when they stay open to 5:00 or 6:00 p.m.. Food stores open on weekdays at 8 a.m. and close at 6:30 p.m.. All shops and banks are closed on national holidays: New Year's, Epiphany, Easter Monday, May Day, Ascension Day, Monday after Pentecost, Corpus Christi Day, Assumption Day, October 26 (National Holiday), All Saints' Day, Immaculate Conception and Christmas (December 25 and 26). Stores in Vienna and Salzburg are invariably more expensive than stores anywhere else in the country. The sales personnel are everywhere very polite and eager to please. Their command of the English language is good in Vienna and Salzburg and usually adequate in other cities.

VAT

The price of every item bought in Austria includes a 20% value-added tax. Foreigners who purchase merchandise costing 1000 ATS or more, are entitled to a refund of the VAT, provided they take the merchandise out of the country unused. Personnel at stores will fill out form U-34, which is validated by an Austrian custom official at your point of departure. From home you mail one copy of the validated form back to the store, which then refunds you the tax. However, this cumbersome process can now be bypassed and a refund received at the point of departure from the country.

Post Office

In Austria post offices handle not only mail but also telegrams, telephones and faxes. They are usually located in the center of town or opposite the railroad station, and are open from 8:00 a.m. to noon and from 2:00 p.m. to 6:00 p.m. on week days only. Stamps are sold not only at post offices but also at *Kiosk*'s (newspaper stands) and tobacco shops. Mail boxes are painted yellow and those from which mail is collected even on Saturdays are marked with a blue stripe. Post offices are equipped with comfortable booths from where long distance calls are made without the use of coins. One pays at a counter after the call, and the calls cost less than one half of what they would at hotels. A convenient alternative for Americans is to sign up for the AT&T USA Direct plan, which makes it possible to call collect from a hotel, or to charge the call to an AT&T credit card. This service is accessed by dialing 022-90-30-11 and is billed like a local call. When calling the US or Canada from Austria, dial 01 followed by the area code and number. If you want to call the UK, dial 044 and the UK telephone number.

Tipping

Hotels include in their bills a service charge of 10% - 15% but it is customary to leave for the maid 25 ATS for each day spent there. She should be additionally tipped for any services out of the ordinary. The concierge will expect to be tipped only for services rendered at your special request such as obtaining theater, opera, or concert tickets, or for reserving a hotel room at your next stop. Porters are given 20 ATS for each piece of luggage they handle plus a tip of at least 10 - 20 ATS. Waiters expect a 10% tip even though a 10 - 15% tip has already been added to your food bill. At hotels, they are tipped on the last day of your stay. A maître d'hôtel who assigned to you an especially desirable table or was very attentive throughout your stay deserves 150 - 200 ATS. Taxi drivers expect a 10% tip, and wardrobe and toilet attendants are given 5 ATS.

HEALTH CONCERNS

The quality of medical care is very good throughout the country, is even better in cities, and is outstanding at hospitals affiliated with medical schools. The medical school in Vienna has been world renowned since the middle of the nineteenth century, and the medical schools in Graz and Innsbruck are also well regarded. Medical expenses of Americans in Austria are not covered at all by Medicare while BC/BS and HMO plans usually cover only treatment for medical emergencies. Even though Medicare does not cover any treatment, some of the Medicare supplemental policies do. One of these is sold by Bankers Life and Casualty Company, 222 Merchandise Mart Plaza, Chicago, IL 60654-2001, Telephone: 312-396-6000. It covers all expenses that Medicare covers in this country, and pays as much as Medicare does here.

Additional temporary health insurance for your trip can be obtained from several, usually small, insurance companies. These policies provide satisfactory insurance for treatment of injuries but only very limited insurance for treatment of illnesses. If you wish to buy any temporary health insurance for your trip, check with a trusted independent insurance broker before calling any of the toll free numbers of unfamiliar insurance companies found in travel magazines. Of the temporary insurance policies we have reviewed, the one offered by Travel Insurance Services, a member of the large and reputable Traveler's Insurance group, seems the most attractive. Address: 2930 Camino Diablo, Suite 200, Box 200, Walnut Creek, CA 94596, Telephone: 1-800-937-1387.

MEASURES

Linear Measures:

m = Me*ter* (meter) = 1.094 yards

cm = *Zentimeter* (centimeter) = 1/100 m = 0.3937 inches

km = *Kilometer* (kilometer) = 1,000 m = 0.6214 miles

Surface Measures:

Hektar (Hectare) = 10,000 square meters = 2.471 acres

Quadratkilometer (square kilometer) = 0.3861 square miles

Capacity Measures:

l = L*iter* (liter) = 1,000 cubic cm = 1.76 pints

Weights:

g = *Gramm* (gram) = 15.4 grains

kg = *Kilogramm* (kilogram) = 1,000 grams = 2.2046 pounds

Temperature:

Temperature is measured in Celsius (Centigrade) units. Water freezes at 0° C and boils at 100° C. To convert Celsius to Fahrenheit units multiply the Celsius figure by 9/5 and add 32. For example:

0° C = 32° F	10°C = 50°F
20°C = 68°F	30°C = 86°F
37°C = 98.6°F	100°C=212°F

TELEPHONE NUMBERS AND ADDRESSES

Emergency Numbers:

- Automobile Breakdown : dial 120

- Fire : dial 122

- Police : dial 133

- Ambulance : dial 144

Embassies:

- U.S.: A-9 Vienna, Boltzmanngasse 16 , Telephone: 0222/31339

- U.K.: A-3 Vienna, Jauresgasse 3, Telephone: 0222/7131575-79

- Canada: A-1 Vienna, Dr-Karl-Lueger-Ring 10, Telephone: 0222/5333691

Information:

- Austria : Österreich Werbung, A-1040 Vienna, Margaretenstraße 1, Telephone: 15872000

- U.S.: Austrian National Tourist Office, Suite 2009, 500 5th Avenue, New York, NY 10110, Telephone: 212-944-6880

- U.K.: Austrian National Tourist Office, 30 St. George Street, London, W1, Telephone: 01-629-0461

- Canada : Austrian National Tourist Office, 2 Bloor Street East, Suite 3330, Toronto, Ontario M4W1AS, Telephone: 416-967-3381

32

VORARLBERG

Vorarlberg is the westernmost province of Austria; its surface area of 2,601 sq. km and population of 315,000 make it the second smallest province. It is bordered by Germany (Bavaria) to the north, Tirol to the east, and Switzerland and Liechtenstein to the south. West of it is the huge Bodensee (Lake Constance) of which only a small part is in Austria while the rest is shared by Germany and Switzerland. The land along the Bodensee and the Rhine River is flat, but most of the province is mountainous and there is world class skiing in the Silvretta area along the Swiss border and at Lech and Zürs, two of Austria's most famous ski resorts.

An oddity of the geography of Vorarlberg is that its Kleines Walsertal (valley) can be reached only through Germany because impassable mountains separate it from the rest of Vorarlberg. In contrast to most other Austrians, who are descendants of the Bavarian tribe, the inhabitants of Vorarlberg descend from the Alemanns, the Germanic tribe that also settled the German speaking parts of Switzerland. The dialect of Vorarlberg still resembles that of Switzerland, and the two populations have many physical and character traits in common. After the breakup of the Habsburg Monarchy in 1918, this sense of kinship was one of the reasons Vorarlberg seriously considered seceding from the new Austrian Republic and joining the Swiss Confederation.

The province is now very prosperous thanks to tourism and industry. Vorarlberg exports huge amounts of hydroelectric power to Germany and also has a strong textile industry concentrated in Dornbirn, the largest city in Vorarlberg.

The international airport nearest to Vorarlberg is in Kloten, near Zurich. The best route from the Zurich airport to the mountains of Vorarlberg and beyond into Tirol is the N3 autobahn from Zurich to near Sagrans, where one takes the N13 autobahn. Cross the Rhine at Buchs and drive through Liechtenstein for 14 km to the Austrian border. The first town in Austria is Feldkirch, and immediately east of this lovely old city is the autobahn A-14, that connects Bregenz with the high mountains of Vorarlberg and Tirol.

Bregenz (population 27,000) is the capital of the province. It lies on the eastern shore of Bodensee (Lake Constance), whose German name comes from the name of a Frankish count who owned much of the land on the northern side of the lake. It derives its English name from the historic

33

city of Konstanz on the western end of the lake. The lake is about 65 km long and up to 12 km wide, and is both fed and drained by the Rhine. The Upper Town of Bregenz was once the stronghold of the counts of Montfort, and sections of its 13th century wall still survive. The city's main landmarks are the large 13th century St. Martin's Tower and the adjacent St. Martin's Chapel built in 1363. Other points of interest in the Upper Town are the Town Hall, the Deuring Schlössle, now a castle hotel, and also a Capuchin Monastery from the 17th century. The Lower Town lies between the Upper Town and the lake and is considerably newer. The New Town Hall was built in 1686, and the adjoining Chapel of St. George in 1408. The latter was rebuilt at the end of the 17th century. There is a very pretty lakeside promenade, a park, a beach, a music pavilion, and the famous Festival Theater with a lakeside amphitheater that seats more than 4,000 spectators and faces a large stage just off shore. It is the site of spectacular open-air opera performances of the Bregenz Music Festival, which takes place every July.

Tourist information on Bregenz can be obtained at the City Tourist Office at Inselstraße 15, Telephone: 05574/23391, and information on the whole province at the Vorarlberg Tourist Office, Römerstraße 7, Telephone: 05574/225250.

DEURING SCHLÖSSLE
A-6900 Bregenz
Ehre-Guta-Platz 4
Telephone: 5574/47800
Fax: 5574/47800-80

The name of the hotel contains the diminutive form of the German word for castle but the hotel is actually a sizable castle on a cliff in the Upper Town from where there are superb views of the lake and the island-city of Lindau, just across the border in Germany.

A castle was built here in the 11th century, was enlarged in the 15th century, and again in the 17th century by a von Deuring. Its garden is full of lush vegetation, and ivy covers the castle to the top of its tower. Inside, there are big beams in the ceilings and old, well-preserved frescos.

The castle became a hotel in 1989, and now has two single and seven double bedrooms, as well as four handsomely decorated suites furnished with many antiques. Much of the hotel's excellent reputation can be attributed to its outstanding restaurant run by Ernst Huber, one of the dozen best cooks in Europe. Double rooms at this four-star hotel cost 1,800 - 2,540 ATS a day, including buffet breakfast. The hotel is open all year and major credit cards are accepted.

Excursions:

A must for anyone vacationing in Bregenz is a trip to the beautiful old German towns of Lindau, Meersburg, Überlingen, and Konstanz, as well as to the island of Mainau and the pilgrimage church in Birnau. Except for Birnau, they can all be reached by boat.

- Lindau, only 8 km by road from Bregenz, is crowded on an island connected to the mainland by a causeway. Its oldest church is the 10th century Peterskirche, where there are rare frescos by Hans Holbein the Elder (1465-1524). There are many other ancient buildings; the Old Town Hall, begun in 1422, is the best preserved. Not far from it is a 13th century church, the location of frequent concerts of church music. The *Marktplatz* (market square) is enclosed by very old houses and two churches, one sternly Gothic and the other cheerfully Baroque. The entrance to the city's picturesque old harbor is guarded by a huge statue of a seated lion, the national symbol of Bavaria.

- Meersburg is about 45 km west of Lindau. When approached by boat on a sunny day, you have a glorious view of the sun-bathed city on a slope rising out of the shimmering lake. In the Upper Town there is an old castle whose main tower was built in 628 by Dagobert, King of the Franks. The castle is private property but its museum, which is open to the public, is well worth seeing. Next to this grim old fortress is an exuberant Baroque palace, *Neues Schloß*, built in the 18th century by the bishop of Konstanz. It is now used for concerts. Behind the two castles, winding cobbled streets lined with half-timbered houses lead to a charming medieval market square, where all houses are neatly painted in pastel colors and decked with window boxes overflowing with brightly colored flowers.

- The pilgrimage church in Birnau is 8-9 km from Meersburg by the coastal road to Überingen. It is on a ledge which offers fine views of the lake and its opposite shore. The church was built in the middle of the 18th century in the Rococo style whose splendour is hidden behind a deceptively plain and colorless façade. Inside, the predominant colors are a tasteful combination of white and gold enlivened by cheerfully bright paintings.

- Then, 3-4 km farther down the lake is the small old city of Überlingen, where the city wall with its seven gates still stands.

- Konstanz is the largest and historically most important city on the Bodensee and is also one of the best preserved medieval cities in

Germany. The most important event in the city's long history was the Council of Konstanz (1414 - 1417). It condemned the efforts of Jan Hus, a Czech theologian, to reform the church and had him burned at the stake as a heretic. This sparked the flame of discontent that later led to the Reformation. The monastery in Konstanz in which Hus was jailed subsequently became a palace. Count Zeppelin, the inventor of air ships, was born there in 1837. The palace is now a superb castle hotel. The Old Town has a lot of charm and has many half-timbered houses going back to the 13th century, but its *Münster* (cathedral) is a dark and melancholy building. It was begun in the 10th and completed only in the 19th century in a mixture of all the intervening building styles.

• A cheerful sight that no visitor to Konstanz should miss is the island of Mainau, 7 km north of the city. The small island reached on foot over a causeway, consists of a hill and a very small stretch of almost flat land. On the summit of the hill is an elegant but unpretentious Baroque castle with a church attached to it. The island and the castle used to belong to the Duke of Baden but passed through marriage to the Swedish royal family. It is now owned and inhabited all year by Count Bernadotte, uncle of the present King of Sweden. Both the old Count and his wife are gardening enthusiasts. Thanks to their efforts over many years, Mainau is now called The Island of Flowers. The unusually warm climate of this island allows many species of flowers to bloom from early spring to late autumn and suits even subtropical vegetation. There are few sights more pleasing to the eye than that of Mainau with its flowers in full bloom.

TIROL

The province of Tirol has a population of about 614,000 and a surface area of 12,647 sq. km.. Since the southern part of the province (*Südtirol*) was ceded to Italy after World War I, Eastern Tirol has been separated from the main body of the province and can be reached only through the province of Salzburg or through Italy. Tirol derives its name from the big old castle Tirol a few kilometers north of Meran (Merano), now in Italy, from where the mighty Counts Vintschgau ruled the province. The red eagle from their coat of arms continues to be the official emblem of Tirol. The capital was moved to Innsbruck in 1420, and after the extinction of the male line of the Counts and later Dukes of Tirol, the province was inherited by the Habsburgs. During the reign of Maximilian I (1490-1519) Innsbruck was for a while the capital of the whole empire.

To the west, Tirol borders on Vorarlberg, to the east on the provinces of Salzburg and Carinthia, to the north on Germany, and to the south on Italy. It is a land of high mountains, deep green valleys, and streams that roll down the mountainsides or plunge with a thundering noise from lofty cliffs. The highest mountain is the Wildspitze (3,772 m) but numerous other peaks are also high enough to be under a permanent cover of snow. The largest river is the Inn which traverses Tirol on the way from its source in Switzerland to the Danube. Some of the land in the valleys is under cultivation but most of it is covered with lush meadows and thick forests, which extend up the mountains to the tree line (about 2,000 m). Above the tree line are the high alpine pastures on which cows lazily graze all summer to the lulling sound of their clanging bells.

Two main roads serve the province. One runs in the east-west direction through most of Austria and connects Tirol with Vorarlberg through a 17 km long tunnel under the Arlberg mountain. The other road runs in the north-south direction from Germany to Italy and carries most of the overland traffic between Central Europe and Italy. A few kilometers south of Innsbruck it crosses the high and graceful *Europabrücke* (bridge) on its way to the *Brenner Paß* (pass) and Italy. Even small secondary roads are well constructed and meticulously maintained, but in the high mountains they may be closed between late fall and the middle of spring.

Visitors are attracted to Tirol not only by the great beauty of its landscape but also by its charming and jovial people. Rosy-cheeked children, *Dirndl*-clad girls and women, and even the stern-looking farmers greet hikers with a cheery *Grüß Gott*. They all proudly wear their colorful garb, happily march to the music of local brass bands, yodel better than anybody else does, and effortlessly go through the acrobatics of the *Schuhplattler* dance.

Innsbruck is in the center of the province, and is the capital of Tirol. This city of about 117,000, lies in the Inn Valley at the intersection of the two most important roads in the province, and as its name (bridge over the Inn) suggests, it has long played an important role in traffic and commerce. The town was founded in 1180, and was a great favorite of Emperor Maximilan I and Empress Maria Theresia. The main tourist attraction is the *Goldenes Dachl*. It is a balcony with a roof of gold-plated copper tiles built in the year 1500 for Emperor Maximilian and his family. From it, they could view in comfort and safety festivities in the small square below. The *Hofkirche* (Court Church) was intended to become Maximilan's mausoleum. In its center is the tomb with a black marble sarcophagus and a bronze figure of the Emperor. The sarcophagus is surrounded by 28 larger-than-life statues of his ancestors, some true and others imagined. At least three of them were designed by Albrecht Dürer. This mausoleum remains the most outstanding work of art in Tirol. Ironically, the Emperor's remains are not there but are in St. George's Church in Wiener Neustadt, south of Vienna. However, another beloved Tirolean leader is buried in this church. When during the Napoleonic Wars Tirol was occupied by French and Bavarian troops, Andreas Hofer, a peasant from the part of Tirol now in Italy, led an uprising against them. At the head of a rag-tag army of peasants he liberated much of Tirol including Innsbruck, but was eventually defeated by the French. Hofer was captured by treachery and was executed, but he has become Austria's most celebrated hero. There are few, if any, towns in Tirol without a monument, a plaque, or a street dedicated to his memory.

The Hofburg, the Imperial Palace in Innsbruck, was built in stages beginning in the 15th century and was completed and redecorated in the Baroque style by Empress Maria Theresia in the 18th century. Its most splendid part is the 30 m long *Riesensaal* (Giants' Hall) whose walls and ceiling are covered with beautiful paintings and portraits of members of the Habsburg family.

The main street in Innsbruck is the wide Maria-Theresien-Straße from which there is an impressive view of towering mountains that seem to be rising straight up out of the city itself.

Innsbruck is also an important center of learning. In addition to a university founded in 1562, it has a medical school whose excellent hospital is within easy driving range from just about anywhere in the province.

Tourist information on Innsbruck and its immediate surroundings can be obtained at the Innsbruck-Igls Tourist Office, A-6021 Innsbruck, Burggraben 3, Telephone: 0512/59850. Information on the whole province is available at Tiroler Werbung, A-6010 Innsbruck, Bozner Platz 6, Telephone: 0512/532059.

HOTEL POST,
SCHLOSS SPRENGENSTEIN
A-6460 Imst
Eduard Wallnöfer-Platz 3
Telephone: 05412/2554
Fax: 05412/251955

The hotel is in the small town of Imst, about 60 km west of Innsbruck, from where it is reached by the A-12 autobahn. The town (elevation 830 m) overlooks the Inn Valley and offers pretty views of the high mountains on the opposite side of the valley.

The building was erected in 1450 by a local businessman who owned the then flourishing mines in the area, but in 1592 it was bought by a nobleman and became a castle. In 1637, however, it was turned into a post office and inn and is, therefore, still known under two names: Hotel Post and Schloß Sprengenstein. It is a large, white, square structure with turrets on its corners and a very large covered terrace on its south side facing the hotel park.

There are 35 spacious, comfortably and tastefully furnished rooms and ten suites, all with large modern baths. The hotel corridors are wide with vaulted ceilings and parquet or tile floors covered with oriental rugs. There are three restaurants of which the rustic one with panelled walls is the most appealing, but the huge covered terrace is everybody's favorite in summer. Food is excellent. There is also a good-sized indoor swimming pool in a separate building in the park. This lovely and elegant hotel with a four-star rating is open February through October. Double rooms with breakfast cost 900 - 1,500 ATS, and half board at an additional 250 ATS per person is a true bargain. All major credit cards are accepted.

Excursions:
The main tourist attraction in this area is the Oetztal, sometimes also spelled Ötztal, a valley that extends from the Inn River all the way to the glaciers on the border with Italy. It is reached by taking the A-12 autobahn towards Innsbruck for only a few kilometers and then turning onto Route 186.

• In the town of Oetz look for a small road on the right marked Piburger See. The road climbs for a couple of kilometers to Piburg, a picture perfect alpine hamlet of neat, centuries old houses decked with flowers. In its center is Gasthof Piburger See, a delightful country inn with a large terrace where one can in peace and comfort sample the simple pleasures of the Austrian cuisine while enjoying a superb view and the clean alpine air. A five minute downhill walk brings one to the Piburger See, a small dark blue lake ringed by woods and mountains. The lake is surprisingly warm and there is a small beach at its far end, reached by a path through a spruce forest so dense that its floor is covered with a thick carpet of always moist moss. This tiny tranquil lake is undoubtedly the most romantic of all the lakes we have seen in the Alps.

• If instead of turning toward Piburg you continue on Route 186, it will take you to the famous ski resorts of Sölden, Obergurgl, and Hochgurgl where there is year-round skiing on a glacier reached by chair lift. Another glacier in the Oetztal can be reached by car. Two kilometers south of Sölden, still on Route 186, take the small road on the right that leads up to the Pitztaler Jöchl (saddle) and ends at a parking lot on the very edge of a large glacier with good facilities for summer skiing.

• Another short car trip takes you to the abbey in Stams. Start again on the autobahn in the direction of Innsbruck but leave it at the second exit, about 18 km from Imst. Follow Route 171 for a couple of kilometers to Stams, where there is a famous Cistercian Abbey, the burial place of the Dukes of Tirol. It was built in the 13th and was enlarged in the 17th and 18th centuries. The church is now a very impressive Baroque building whose pastel colored exterior is plain, but the interior is sumptuously decorated with a perhaps excessive amount of gold.

Tirol

JAGDSCHLOSS KÜHTAI
A-6183 Kühtai
Telephone: 05239/201
Fax: 05239/281

Jagdschloß Kühtai is reached from Innsbruck by driving west on the A-12 autobahn for 11 km. At the Kematen exit take the well-marked road to Gries in the scenic Sellrain Valley. The road climbs more perceptively after Gries and at 25 km from Kematen reaches its highest point (2,017 m). The hotel is just beyond this point in the midst of alpine pastures and mountain peaks of up to 3,016 m. This area is popular with hikers in summer and with skiers in winter. Snow conditions are good throughout the winter months and there are many cross-country and downhill trails that satisfy the needs of both beginners and experts. The hotel was for centuries a hunting lodge of the Habsburg family. It was built by Archduke Leopold in 1625 on the site of a smaller 13th century building and is presently owned by Count Stolberg-Stolberg, a great-grandson of Emperor Franz Josef.

The hotel is a squat rectangular building with a 17th century chapel next to it. The light colored walls of the hotel are enlivened by delicate paintings above the windows and by shutters with red and white stripes. Inside, some public areas have vaulted ceilings while in others both walls and ceilings are panelled with knotted pine. There are many valuable antiques but also some simple, charmingly rustic furniture that contributes to the ambiance of an aristocratic hunting lodge. The hotel has nine suites and 36 rooms with baths. It has a four-star rating. Double rooms cost 1,160 - 1,650 ATS including half board. American Express and Diners cards are accepted. The hotel is unfortunately open only during the winter season, from December through April.

Excursions:
• In winter, skiers staying at this hotel can take advantage of the famous ski resorts in the nearby Oetztal Valley. The town of Oetz is only 16 km west of the hotel and from there, continue on Route 186 to Sölden, Vent, and Obergurgl. Sölden is by far the largest of the three ski resorts and has many ski lifts including the highest lift in Austria, which takes skiers to the Geislacher Kogl (3,058 m). Vent (elevation 1896 m), the smallest of the three resorts, is secluded at the end of a long valley, and it is its remotness that helped Vent win a place in history. For, when the ruler of Tirol, Duke Friedrich was deposed in

a coup in 1415, he sought refuge from his pursuers in the valley of Vent, the poorest and most inaccessible area of Tirol. Despite the substantial reward for his capture and the risk to their own lives, the destitute peasants of Vent kept him hidden until he was restored to power. The grateful Duke then decreed that inhabitants of this valley would never again have to pay any taxes. Difficult as it may be nowadays to believe it, his promise was honored by subsequent rulers for more than four centuries, until 1850.

• Obergurgl (1910 m) is a famous ski resort a short distance from Vent. It has the distinction of beeing the highest parish in Austria.

• In summer there are good hiking trails to the nearby three Plenderles Lakes and the big Finstertal Stausee, and we recommend these excursions to guests at Schloß Sprengenstein, the Grünwalderhof, and Schloß Igls.

HOTEL GRÜNWALDERHOF
A-6082 Patsch
Römerstraße 1
Telephone: 512/37304
Fax: 512/378078

The Grünwalderhof is in Patsch, a small village at an elevation of 1,000 m, only a few kilometers south of Innsbruck. Coming from the direction of Innsbruck on the A-13 autobahn, usually referred to as the *Brenner Autobahn*, take the second exit. The road forks 2 km from the exit. Take the road to the left, and you will immediately see the hotel on a hill on the left side at the far end of a large, gently rising meadow. As the hotel's address indicates, it is on a road built by the Romans. This now quiet, small road was for many centuries the main road over the Brenner Pass. The present hotel building used to be a stagecoach station, part of the Austrian mail and stagecoach monopoly owned by the Princes Thurn und Taxis. When the postal service was nationalized in the 19th century, the building became a hunting lodge and was only recently converted into a hotel. Its present owner, the Count Thurn und Taxis, still resides in it. The hotel is a rectangular building to which a small wing has been added. On the side facing the road a large crest of the owner's family has been

47

painted, and there are also small decorative paintings around the windows. On the side of the hotel facing south there is a large terrace shared by several rooms, and on the floor above it, a sizable balcony with a pair of huge antlers under the gable. The panelled walls of the main hall are hung with hunting trophies, prints, and old maps, and genuine stagecoach memorabilia are present in all other public areas. The most attractive part of the hotel is the centuries old dining room with panelled walls, a wood ceiling, and antique wood furniture. Stagecoach passengers rested here, ate, and soaked up heat before continuing their journey. There are only four tables in this charming little room, where one dines by candlelight. Most guests are served in a larger, more modern, and much less attractive dining room. In summer, lunch and dinner are also served on a grassy terrace behind the hotel. From there, a view unfolds of the stunningly beautiful alpine world extending from the meadow at the edge of the terrace across the valley of the Sill River deep below, to the far-off glaciers of the Stubai Alps. Guests whose rooms have balconies can savor this view in comfort at any time of the day and on weekends can also admire the skill of paragliders who jump off the nearby 2,247 m high Patscherkofel, gracefully float in the blue sky and land on the mark on the soft meadow next to the hotel.

An outdoor pool, a small indoor pool, and a tennis court are available to the guests.

The hotel's three-star rating does not give it all the credit it deserves for the exceptionally pretty location. There are 21 rooms furnished with solid furniture. They all have private baths but some tubs are small. The price of a double room with buffet breakfast is 990 - 1,420 ATS a day for stays of at least three nights and slightly more for shorter stays. We strongly recommend signing up for half board as its cost is very reasonable and the four course dinners are outstanding.

The hotel is open between May and October and again from December through March. Payment in cash is preferred, but Visa and American Express cards are accepted.

The location of this hotel is superb, the food outstanding, the ambiance pleasant, and the price very reasonable.

Excursions:

- There are five picturesque alpine valleys between Patsch and the Brenner Pass. The first and largest is the Stubaital, which begins at Schönberg, the first exit from the autobahn after Patsch. The road passes through Neustift, then narrows considerably and continues along the foaming Ruetz Bach (brook) up to Mutterberg Alm (pasture) which is 46 km from the autobahn. A cable car will whisk you from there up to the Dresdner Hütte (hut), where you can take any of a number of hiking trails that intersect there, or continue by cable car to the top station at 2,900 m. From here, ski lifts take skiers up the glacier on which one can ski even in summer.

* The other four valleys on the way to the Brenner Pass are the Navis, Geschnitz, Vals, and Obernberg Valleys. They are well off the tourist track and still have quaint hamlets idylically set against a backdrop of lush pastures, woods, and precipitous cliffs. In these valleys it is best to drive along the brook that runs through each of them to the end of the road, from where trails lead into the mountains. In the Obernbergtal there is a pretty lake, the Obernberger See, reached by an easy 45 minute walk from the inn at the end of the road. All these valleys are only a short distance from one another, and two of them can easily be explored in a single day. They are reached either by way of the autobahn or by driving from the hotel on the narrow but scenic road through the villages of Patsch and Elbögen to Matrei. This road winds its way very high above the Sill Valley and is so narrow that when two cars meet, one has to stop slightly off the road for the other to pass. In the center of Patsch there are large, sturdy, lovingly maintained old houses. Their white walls are adorned with paintings of saints, and their windows are decked with geraniums. Many houses are also inscribed with the date when they were acquired by the present owners, and a surprising number of them appear to have been owned by the same family since the 17th century. The hillside road from Patsch joins Route 182 in Matrei am Brenner, and this road will take you to the previously mentioned valleys directly under the Brenner Pass.

* Sightseeing and shopping trips to Innsbruck are best saved for cloudy days, which from time to time occur even in the relatively dry months of June, September, and October. It is much more convenient to make the trip by bus than by car. There is a bus stop at the hotel from which busses leave almost every hour. They are modern, spacious, and clean and cost much less than parking in the city does. The ride takes slightly more than half an hour and ends at the bus terminal at the Innsbruck railroad station only minutes from the center.

The Stubai Alps

•   Finally, there is a walk that all hotel guests should take at least once. A short time before sunset, take the footpath at the end of the parking lot and follow it as it climbs a small hill 5 minutes from the hotel. One side of the hill is covered with a thick pine and spruce forest and the other with grass. From its top, a majestic view unfolds of the Alps with forests, pastures, jagged mountain ridges, and plunging valleys. The snow-capped peaks and glaciers of the Stubai Alps at that time of the day still glisten in the glare of the setting sun, but darkness has already enveloped the valleys and gradually creeps up the mountainsides. Cows on the pastures are only barely visible, and even the distant clanging of their bells is dying away. Soon, perfect stillness reigns except for the soothing chirping of crickets, which only enhances the awe-inspiring, unworldly quiet that pervades the air.

For other excursions please see Schloß Igls, Schloß Sprengenstein, and Jagdschloß Kühtai.

SCHLOSSHOTEL IGLS
A-6080 Igls
Viller Steig 2
Telephone: 0512/377217
Fax: 0512/378679

The small town of Igls is only a few kilometers south of Innsbruck from where it can be reached by a 20 minute tram ride or by bus which then continues up to Patsch. The hotel is at an elevation of 900 meters, in its own small park bordering on pastures. It offers gorgeous views of the Karwendel Range to the north and the Patscherkofel mountain immediately to the south. Innsbruck, way down in the Inn Valley, is out of sight.

The castle was built in the 19th century and was used mostly as a summer residence until its present owners, Dr. and Mrs. Beck, had it extensively renovated and rebuilt in the 1960's after which the castle became a luxury hotel.

It is a distinguished looking, castle-like, white building that radiates quiet prosperity and restrained elegance. The hotel is in the five-star category and has 20 splendid guest rooms and suites, which like all the public rooms are airy, elegant, tastefully decorated, and very comfortably furnished in the traditional style. A sumptuous Royal Suite is at this time nearing completion. The hotel boasts all the contemporary amenities including a spectacular indoor-outdoor swimming pool, a fitness center, and a tennis court. Golfing and skiing are available in the immediate vicinity. A double room with half board costs 3,600 - 4,500 ATS. The hotel is open from January through March and from June through September. Major credit cards are accepted.

Excursions:

- The base station of the cable car to the Patscherkofel is only minutes from the hotel. In winter the cable car provides easy access to excellent ski trails, and in summer it enables even the less active to reach the top of the mountain and behold the glory of distant peaks and glaciers. It takes one up to the elevation of 1,952 m, and a chair lift continues up to the summit (2,246 m) from where there are spectacular views. To the north is the Zugspitze, which at 2,961 m is the highest peak in Germany; to the northeast is Achensee and behind it the 2,299 m high Rofan group; to the southeast, the Tuxer and the Zillertaler Alps, whose peaks reach over 3,500 m; and to the southwest the Stubai Alps, which soar to 3,507 m. On the way back, you may get off the cable car at Heiligwasser, an intermediate station. A small church clings there to the steep mountain, and next to it is a spring whose crystal clear, ice cold mountain water is said to effect miraculous cures (*Heiligwasser* means holy water). A wide path through woods leads back to Igls.

- A delightful whole day trip to Linderhof Palace in Bavaria begins with a drive to Plansee, the second largest lake in Tirol. Take the A-12 autobahn west to Telfs, 27 km from Innsbruck, and continue on Route 189, which climbs high above the valley of the Inn and affords pretty views of the valley and of the Stubai Alps across it. In Nassereith turn right onto Route 314, which takes you over the Fern Paß and by several small lakes. To your right is the towering massive of the Zugspitze. At Reutte, turn right onto the road marked Plansee. The lake is about 6 km long and the hamlet of Plansee is at its far end. In a small square near the entrance to the beach stands a monument to a 19th century Bavarian king, which is surprising in view of the longstanding animosity between the Tiroleans and the Bavarians. An old man in worn Tirolean garb offered an explanation according to which a long spell of drought in the 19th century had caused misery and hunger in Tirol. This King of the neighboring Bavaria took pity on the suffering peasants and invited them to cross the border into Bavaria, where conditions were better. When the Tiroleans later returned home, they erected this monument to the King, who was so moved by their gratitude that he had a road built between Plansee and Bavaria. The old man concluded with the observation that there had obviously been cooperation among European countries long before the European Union.

• The road he was referring to takes you to Linderhof Palace, 17 km away, in Bavaria (Germany). Schloß Linderhof is the most beautiful of the many castles built by King Ludwig II of Bavaria. As palaces go, it is modest in size, certainly much smaller than Neuschwanstein, King Ludwig's more famous fantasy castle almost as bogus as its Disney lookalike. Linderhof, however, is genuine, a small but well-proportioned Rococo palace, resplendent but not showy. It fits superbly into its surroundings but is outdone in beauty by its huge, magnificently landscaped park. Facing the palace is a pool with a large decorative fountain that shoots the highest jet of water in Germany, and behind the pool is a slope with terraced formal gardens and a multitude of statues, urns, and vases full of brightly colored flowers. A graceful stairway majestically rises from one terrace to the next, and the view from the highest terrace down on the palace and the artificial cascade behind it is simply fabulous.

For other excursions please see Schloß Sprengenstein, Jagdschloß Kühtai, and the Hotel Grünwalderhof.

FÜRSTENHAUS
A-6213 Pertisau am Achensee
Telephone: 05243/5442
Fax: 05243/6168

Fürstenhaus is in a quiet lakeside location on the west shore of Achensee, the largest lake in Tirol. To the east are the Rofangebirge (mountain range), and to the west rise the wild Karwendelgebirge (mountain range). Coming by car on the A-12 autobahn, take the Jenbach exit, 39 km east of Innsbruck, and continue on Route 181 in the northerly direction. The road winds up a large and steep slope. At its last and sharpest turn there is a parking lot. Stop for a minute for a panoramic view of a large portion of Tirol including the pretty Zillertal Valley and the snowy mountain peaks at its far end. A few kilometers farther up the road, in Maurach, turn left to Pertisau, which is 7 km away.

Fürstenhaus is a large, square dwelling in the local Alpine style. It is white with red and white shutters like those of fortified castles. A very long and considerably lower new wing extends from the main building along the lake. The original building was erected by Duke Sigismund of Tirol in 1469 and became the favorite fishing and hunting lodge of Emperor Maximilian in 1490. It was turned into a hotel in 1853 and was completely renovated and expanded in 1980. There are now 59 double rooms and one suite, all with modern bathrooms and many also with balconies. There is a spacious hall with a fireplace, two dining rooms, a terrace, a greenhouse, an indoor pool, a sauna, and a fitness and beauty center. The hotel has its own nine hole golf course and a private beach where sail boats can be rented. The base station of a ski lift is only minutes away. It takes one to the ski area on the 1,491 m high Zwölferkopf. Pertisau is also a renowned cross-country ski center with 75 km of well groomed cross-country ski trails.

This four-star hotel is open between the middle of December and the beginning of April, and again from May to the end of October. Double rooms with half board cost 2,600 - 3,100 ATS, and major credit cards are honored.

Excursions:

- A well maintained, wide walking trail leads to Grammai Alm (pasture), which is about 9 km west of Pertisau and can also be reached by car. From there, a hiking trail continues for about 3 km to Lamsenjoch Hütte (hut) and on into the essentially untouched wilderness of the Karwendel Reservation.

- The charming Alpbach Valley and the medieval city of Rattenberg can easily be toured in a single day. Drive on Route 181 down into the Inn Valley. After crossing the river, turn left onto Route 171 to Brixlegg, where you make a right turn onto the road to Reith and Alpbach. The village of Alpbach is 10.5 km from Brixlegg in the bucolic Alpbach Valley surrounded by gently rising wooded mountains. The small village smothered in alpine beauty and virtually drowning in a sea of flowers was not long ago officially declared the most beautiful village in Austria. From there, you can either walk or drive along the Alpbach (brook) to the even more secluded Inner Alpbach from where two easy hiking trails continue up into the mountains. After retracing your way to Brixlegg, turn right onto Route 171 and continue about 2 km to Rattenberg. Leave the car in the parking lot at the entrance to this medieval city and continue on foot. The small city is hemmed in between the Inn River and a cliff on which stands a castle ruin. The whole city is only 300 m long and consists of a few narrow streets connected by even narrower lanes. The most noteworthy building is the Gothic church built in 1473 but redecorated in the Baroque style in the 18th century.

Alpbach

•   A day trip into the high Alps also begins with a drive from the hotel down to the Inn and continues on Route 169 through the Zillertal Valley and the resort town of Mayrhofen. A couple of kilometers beyond it bear right into the scenic Tuxertal. At the upper end of the valley is Hintertux, a hamlet very popular with summer skiers. A cable car or a hiking trail will take you from the village up to Sommerberg Alm (pasture). Skiers continue by cable car and several chair lifts to the glaciers at an elevation of about 3,000 m, and hikers continue from Sommerberg on foot to the Tuxer Joch (Saddle) at 2,338 m, from where there is a stunning view of the whole area. Just below the saddle is the Tuxer Joch Haus, about 2 hours on foot from Hintertux. From its sunny terrace there are breathtaking views of huge glaciers and the jagged snow-covered peaks of Hoher Riffler (3,231 m), Olperer (3,476 m), and Kl. Kaserer (3,093 m). A path behind the hut leads past a pretty cascade on the left and the impressive Schlererfall (waterfall) on the right side down to Hintertux.

HOTEL SCHLOSS LEBENBERG
A-6370 Kitzbühel
Lebenbergstraße 17
Telephone: 05356/4301
Fax: 05356/4405

Kitzbühel is about 100 km northeast of Innsbruck and is best reached by the A-12 autobahn that connects Munich and Innsbruck. After leaving the autobahn at Wörgl, 57 km from Innsbruck, take Route 312 and after about 4 km cross the Brixenthaler Ache (river) on your right, then turn left onto Route 170. A few kilometers down the road you will pass by Schloß Itter, a charming little castle on the summit of a wooded hill on the left. Kitzbühel is 29 km from Wörgl, and Schloß Lebenberg is a short distance before Kitzbühel, on the left, situated on a sunny terrace above the town.

Built in the 16th century, Schloß Lebenberg has since changed hands many times and is now a four-star hotel with 109 rooms and suites, neatly furnished in a style that blends the traditional with the contemporary. The hotel has five prize-winning restaurants, tennis courts, an indoor swimming pool, a fitness center, and a beauty center of which they are particularly proud. Schloß Lebenberg offers a historical setting, refined personal comfort, and up-to-date recreational facilities at a moderate price. At the height of the summer season double rooms cost up to 3,120 ATS a day including buffet breakfast and an elegant four course dinner. At Christmas time, the price is about 500 ATS higher, but in May, June, and September, it is about 500 ATS lower than in the main season. The hotel is open all year and major credit cards are accepted.

Excursions:

- Free bus rides are provided to Kitzbühel and the nearby ski slopes. The most interesting part of Kitzbühel is the Old Town whose main streets are the Vorderstadt and Hinterstadt Streets lined with old gabled houses with large paintings on their walls. There are three 14th and 15th century churches on Vorderstadt Street, all well worth a visit.

- There are good hiking trails on the Hahnenkamm (1,665 m) and the Kitzbühler Horn (1,998 m) which are reached by lifts. On the summit of the Kitzbühler Horn are a chapel, a restaurant, and a park in which virtually all alpine plants are represented.

- Kitzbühel is one of the most prestigious ski resorts in the world. The best known of its ski trails is the 3.5 km long very steep Hahnenkamm Run of Olympic fame.

SCHLOSS MÜNICHAU
A-6370 Kitzbühel
Reith 32
Telephone: 05356/2962

Schloß Münichau is within walking distance of Schloß Lebenberg and is only 3.5 km northwest of Kitzbühel, from where it is reached by driving on Route B-170 toward Kirchberg. After 2.5 km, turn right onto the small road toward Reith. The castle is beside the road on the right side.

It is a tall white structure with a tower, surrounded by fields behind which the saw toothed peaks of the Wild Kaiser jut skyward.

The castle was built in 1469 by Wilhelm von Münichawe, later called Münichauer. It changed hands several times and around the year 1600 was inherited by the mighty von Lamberg family in whose possession it remained for three centuries. It was destroyed by lightening in 1914 and was sold in 1921. Its present owners rebuilt the castle in 1957, carefully restored it to its original condition, and made it a hotel. The castle's Knights' Hall is now a congenial dining room with a rustic stove, a tiled floor, and a pretty wood ceiling. Its walls are hung with hunting trophies and old weapons. Stone-framed arched doors, vaulted ceilings, and a very pretty old chapel on the second floor contribute to the ambiance of this small castle. The 35 guest rooms are of good size and are furnished with new but rustic-looking furniture. The bathrooms are modern but somewhat small, while the elevators are definitely confining.

The hotel is open all year except in November. Its rating is unfortunately unavailable at this time. The price of double rooms with half board is between 900 and 2,400 ATS depending on the room and the season. Major credit cards are accepted.

Excursions:
    See Schloß Lebenberg.

NOTE: *According to information just received, the hotel's present rating no longer meets our minimum standard.*

SALZBURGER LAND
(Salzburg Province)

The Province of Salzburg is 7,155 sq. km large and has a population of 465,000. It borders on Germany (Bavaria) to the northwest, the Province of Upper Austria to the north and northeast, Styria to the east, Carinthia, East Tirol, and Italy to the south, and Tirol to the west. It is a land of great geographical diversity with high mountains, forests, lakes, and quaint villages which contrast with the urbane sophistication of its capital. East of the city is the area of Salzkammergut where most of the salt consumed in central Europe used to be mined. Thanks to its pretty lakes, the Salzkammergut has become a popular summer resort area shared by the provinces of Salzburg, Upper Austria, and Styria. South of the city of Salzburg the province is mountainous, and its southern border runs through the Hohe Tauern Mountains, the highest mountain range in Austria. Their highest peak, the Großglockner, is just across the line in Carinthia. At the foot of the Großlockner is the warm Zeller See, and in the center of the province is the Liechtensteinklamm, one of the most impressive gorges in the Alps. Not far from this gorge is Badgastein, one of Europe's most famous spas.

Badgastein

At the western end of the province, near its border with Tirol, is the highest waterfall in Europe, the Krimmler Wasserfälle.

The **City of Salzburg**, population 140,000, is the capital of the province. It is at the northern end of the province and only a few kilometers from the German border. The city is at the foothills of the Alps, huddled between the Mönchsberg and the Nonnberg(mountains) in the south and the Kapuzinerberg in the north. The Salzach River divides it into the smaller *Altstat* (Old Town), crowded between the Mönchsberg and the left bank of the river, and the newer part of town on the right bank. The city is dominated by the Hohensalzburg Fortress, the largest fully preserved medieval fortress in Europe. It was built between the years 1077 and 1500, and from it the Prince Archbishops of Salzburg ruled over their independent state until 1803. Toward the end of that period, the Archbishops did not actually inhabit the fortress but lived in a palace in the city or in one of the smaller palaces near Salzburg.

The twisting cobbled streets of the Old Town are lined with tall and narrow centuries old houses. In its center is the *Residenz* (palace of the Archbishop), built at the turn of the 16th century and now open to the public. In front of it, in the Residenzplatz, is a 15 m high marble fountain and on the opposite side of the square a 17th century palace for the Archbishop's guests. Its tower houses the *Glockenspiel*, whose bells play

Hohensalzburg

Mozart tunes at 7:00 am, 11:00 am, and 6:00 pm, and attract numerous tourists. On the southern side of the square is the huge 17th century Dom (cathedral). The very old and narrow Getreidegasse is both the prettiest and the busiest street in the Old Town. At its eastern end is the Old Town Hall, and farther down on the right is the 13th century *Alter Markt* (Old Market) in which there is a pharmacy that goes back to the 16th century.

The Hohensalzburg Fortress is best reached by the *Festungsbahn* (funicular) whose base station is next to the ancient St. Peter's Cemetery in which there are early Christian catacombs. The fortress now houses several museums and provides sweeping views of the town and its surroundings. On the way back to the city, take the foot path. A small detour from it will take you to the ancient Nonnberg Convent founded in the year 700.

In the newer part of Salzburg on the right bank of the river is the Mirabell Palace, built in 1606 by Prince Archbishop Dietrich von Raitenau for his mistress with whom he fathered 15 children. The palace garden is undoubtedly the most beautiful in Salzburg, and from its far end there is a superb view of the cheerful park full of bright flowers against the backdrop of the colossal Hohensalzburg Fortress.

Tourist information can be obtained at the Salzburg City Tourist Office at Mozart Platz 5, Telephone: 0662/847568.

HOTEL JAGDSCHLOSS GRAF RECKE
A-5742 Wald im Oberpinzgau
Telephone: 06565/6417
Fax: 06565/6920

The hotel is just outside the village of Wald im Oberpinzgau, in the Salzach Valley, at the foot of a mountain range dominated by the towering 3,674 m high Großvenediger. It is reached from Salzburg by driving on the A-10 autobahn south to Bischofshofen and then west along the Salzach River on Route 311, a good road which after awhile becomes Route 168, and finally Route 165. To reach the hotel from the opposite side, from Innsbruck, take the A-12 autobahn to Jenbach and then Route 169 through the Zillertal Valley. In Zell am Ziller, pick up Route 165. After quite a few hairpin turns, this steadily climbing road leads over the Gerlospaß and then descends into the Salzach Valley and continues through the village of Wald. At the end of the village on the left is a small road with a sign pointing to the hotel nestled in a tranquil alpine setting at the far end of a very pretty meadow.

There was a fortified castle on this spot in the Middle Ages. On its foundation an ancestor of the present owner built a hunting lodge early in this century. This was turned into a hotel in the 1970's, but much of

Salzburg Province

the ambiance of a hunting lodge was preserved. The 19 rooms and the 4 suites are comfortable and rather modern. The lounge is replete with hunting trophies and family memorabilia under which the owner and manager, Dr. Count von der Recke, likes to entertain his guests with stories about his hunting trips. Food is good and is offered in generous proportions in a contemporary dining room or on a very pretty terrace. An air of friendliness and congeniality permeates this cozy four-star hotel. The price of double rooms with half board is 1,540 to 2,100 ATS. The hotel is open from June to October and from December through March. American Express, Visa, and Diners cards are accepted.

Excursions:

- The Jagdschloß is ideally located for most outdoor activities, and the Count will gladly advise you about hikes through the nearby National Park. He can also help hunters make arrangements for hunting in a 20,000 acre hunting preserve, direct anglers to the best trout streams, and tennis players, golfers and horseback riders to the nearest facilities.

- The main tourist attraction in the area is the Krimmler Wasserfälle, the highest waterfall in Europe, where the Krimmler Ache plunges 380 m over 3 waterfalls. The waterfalls are about 10 km west of the hotel on Route 165. A 30-minute walk from the parking lot through a cool spruce forest takes one to the lowest fall. The highest is about 1 hour up a wide but fairly steep path which offers breathtaking views to those who stop to catch their breath. It is difficult to tell whether the sight of each waterfall is more impressive from below or from above it.

- In winter, downhill skiers have a choice of 30 ski lifts in the vicinity of the hotel, and 40 km of groomed trails await cross-country skiers.

SCHLOSS PRIELAU
A-5700 Zell am See
Hofmannsthalstraße
Telephone: 06542/2609
Fax: 06542/260955

Schloß Prielau is 85 km from Salzburg, from where it is reached by the A-10 autobahn to Bischofshofen and Route 311 to Zell am See. Follow the same road through the town and along the west shore of the Zeller See to the end of the lake, where you make a right turn onto a smaller road that continues around the lake. Schloß Prielau is on the left side, about one kilometer from Route 311.

Built in the year 1560 by a baronial family, it later belonged to the church and is now owned by the von Hofmannsthal family. After extensive renovation, the castle recently became a hotel. Schloß Prielau is a large, square building with a steeply pitched shingled roof and is flanked by two towers. It is painted white and its window shutters, red and white, the colors of Austria. It is set in its own park next to a small Baroque church, a trout farm, a deer farm, and a tennis court. The hotel's lakeside beach is 300 m away, and 5 km away is a 27 hole golf course where hotel guests are given a green fee discount of 20%.

This castle is a gem. Everything in it is in mint condition, and obviously no money or effort is spared to keep it so. Some ceilings are vaulted while others have exposed beams. There are nice wood and marble floors, cozy tiled stoves, and numerous antiques. In the graceful dining room oriental rugs cover the marble floor, and attractivelly presented gourmet food is elegantly served.

There are 10 guest rooms in the castle proper and a few more in an adjacent building. They are comfortably furnished with neat new but rustic looking furniture. Views from all rooms are pretty, but views from the rooms in the eastern tower are stunning. To the north and east are beautiful mountains and fields dotted with yellow flowers, to the south is the tranquil lake, and beyond it are the snowy peaks of the highest mountains in Austria. Bathrooms are large and have all the modern amenities including floor heating.

The hotel has a four-star rating and is open from December through October. Double rooms with half board cost 2,700 - 3,800 ATS. Major credit cards are accepted.

Excursions:

- A trip to the Großglockner, the highest mountain in the country, begins with a ride back on Route 311 to Bruck and the Großglockner Hochalpenstraße. This 47 km long marvel of engineering with hair-rasing hairpin turns reaches its highest point (2,500 m) in a tunnel. Seven kilometers past the tunnel, now in the province of Carinthia, turn right onto the Gletscherstraße which continues for a few kilometers to the Franz-Josephs-Höhe. From that point, there is a glorious view of the glittering snow covered peak of the Großglockner (3,797 m), proudly rearing in center stage, and of the Pasterze Gletscher (glacier) far below. The glacier is 9 km long and 1.5 km wide. Its shape and corrugated surface make it look like a mighty river solidly frozen since time immemorial. It is reached by a funicular or on foot, passing by the Hofmanns Hütte, a hut that clings to the sheer cliff high above the glacier.

- In winter, a short ride in a gondola takes skiers from Zell am See to the Schmittenhöhe (2,000 m), where there is excellent skiing. Five kilometers south of Zell am See is Kaprun, a famous ski resort. Its Kitzsteinhorn (3,203 m) has a large glacier on which one can ski all year. In summer, one can ski there in the morning and swim in the warm Zeller See in the afternoon. Zell am See and Kaprun together feature 55 lifts, 130 km of downhill, and 200 km of cross-country trails.

Additional suggestions for excursions are found in the sections on Jagdschloß Graf Recke and Schloß Haunsperg.

SCHLOSS HAUNSPERG
A-5411 Oberalm bei Hallein
Telephone: 06245/2662
Fax: 06245/5680

Schloß Haunsperg is less than 20 km south of Salzburg, just north of the small town of Hallein.

The existence of this estate was first recorded in the year 1365. In 1388 it belonged to the Haunsperg family whose name the castle still carries. The history of the building is less certain, but the main tower certainly goes back to the middle ages while most of the castle and its chapel were built in the early part of the 17th century. The property was extensively renovated in 1960 and its owners, the charming von Gernerth family, now run the castle as a small hotel.

It is an almost square building flanked by two towers and a large Baroque chapel. There is a tennis court next to the chapel, and a pretty park with big old trees surrounds the whole castle complex. The hotel has two single and two double rooms , as well as six suites which, as is customary in small castle hotels, are identified by name rather than by number. The public rooms and the very spacious guest rooms are almost completely furnished with fine antiques and decorated with oil paintings, old photographs, and a miscellany of vases, medals, and other interesting knickknacks. The handsome parquet floors are covered with oriental rugs and there is a grand piano in the music room. The inside of the chapel is decorated with 17th century stucco ornaments and some 30 frescos from the same period. This four-star hotel is open all year and major credit cards are accepted. The cost of a double room is 1,700 - 1,900 ATS a day including buffet breakfast served in a very impressive breakfast room on the ground floor. There is no restaurant at the hotel, but the amiable owners will gladly advise you about restaurants in the vicinity.

Excursion:

• The hotel's proximity to Salzburg makes it a convenient base for sightseeing and shopping in the city.

• A day trip to the Liechtensteinklamm (gorge) begins on the A-10 autobahn at Hallein. About 30 km south of there, on the right side, is Schloß Hohenwerfen, an awsome, big and grim castle on a cliff above the Salzach River. At the Bischofshofen exit from the autobahn take Route 311 and after about nine kilometers cross the Salzach into St. Johann im Pongau and follow the signs to Liechtensteinklamm, 5 km south of the town. The gorge was carved over the millennia by the Großarl Bach and ranks among the grandest gorges in the Alps. Its walls are up to 300 m high while the gorge at several points is less than 4 m wide. The path through it, partly blasted from the rock, clings to the cliff or crisscrosses the gushing torrent before ending at the foot of a 60 m high waterfall.

• Another enjoyable day trip is to the nearby Königssee in Bavaria. Take Route 159 north. At its junction with Route 150 turn left and continue on this road as it first becomes Route 160 and after crossing into Germany becomes Route 305. Then, 14 km from the border turn left onto Route 20 to Königssee, a few kilometers away. The 8 km long dark blue lake is in the center of a large national park and is encircled by high mountains. At the northern end of the lake, board one of the small, electrically driven excursion boats for a remarkably quiet ride that affords an excellent view of the entire lake and its surroundings. At a certain point during the ride the skipper will blow a bugle at a sheer cliff on the right side of the lake and invite the passengers to count how many times the echo bounces back and forth across the lake. The first stop is at a peninsula accessible only by boat. Its main attractions are the pretty 17th century St. Bartholomä

Chapel and a former hunting lodge converted into a very pleasant tavern. The next and last stop is at the far end of the lake from where a path leads to the much smaller but picturesque Obersee.

For other excursions, please see Schloß Prielau and Schloß Fuschl.

SCHLOSSHOTEL ST. RUPERT
A-5020 Salzburg
Marzger Straße3
Telephone: 0662/820084
Fax: 0662/832217

This castle hotel is only 5 minutes by car south of Salzburg. It is surrounded by its own large park from where the outline of the Hohensalzburg Fortress is seen through the crowns of centuries old trees. The castle's existence was first recorded in 1540, when it was a summer residence of the Prince Archbishop of Salzburg. It was named after an early bishop and patron saint of Salzburg who converted the population of the area to Christianity. At one time it was the seat of the Order of The Knights of St. Rupert and was later owned by various nobles. The castle has been a hotel since 1929 and was completely renovated in 1966. It is a large Baroque building painted yellow with white trimmings, while its roof and window shutters are green. The hotel has 30 spacious individually decorated and comfortably furnished guest rooms. Some public rooms have vaulted ceilings supported by stone columns, tile floors with oriental rugs; and one of them is adorned with a glazed tile stove bearing the likenesses of the twelve apostles and the crests of the provinces of the former empire. This four star hotel is open from December through October. Double rooms with half board cost 4,460 ATS in summer and 4,060 in winter. The cuisine is classic Austrian with desserts like Kaiserschmarrn, Topfenpalatschinken, and Salzburger Nockerln. Major credit cards are accepted.

Excursions:

Salzburg is easily reached on foot or by bicycle, which can be obtained at the hotel. To get there, turn left on the quiet and scenic Hellbrunner Allee behind the hotel. If instead of turning left you turn right, Hellbrunner Allee will take you to the nearby Schloß Hellbrunn. This castle is open to the public and is famous for its park and a small zoo.

For other suggestions, please see Schloß Prielau, Schloß Haunsperg, and Schloß Fuschl.

SCHLOSS LEOPOLDSKRON
A-5020 Salzburg
Leopoldskronstraße 56-58
Telephone: 0662/83983
Fax: 0662/83983-7

Schloß Leopoldskron is 20 to 30 minutes on foot south of Salzburg's Old Town and almost directly under the Hohensalzburg Fortress. This serene Baroque palace, built between 1736 and 1740 by the then reigning Prince Archbishop, is in a large English park with big old trees, gravel paths, and lovely lawns with Baroque statues. A romantic lake behind the palace completes the idyllic picture. Since 1947 Leopoldskron has been the site of the Salzburg Seminars whose purpose is the exchange of views on international problems in politics, science, and culture. It became a hotel only very recently, has not yet received an official rating, but is unlikely to be awarded less than four stars.

In the very impressive main building are an elegant Baroque hall used only on special occasions, seminar facilities, and six spacious, attractively furnished suites with superb views of the lake and the park. The suites have big old glazed stoves, which are occasionally used. All other guest rooms are in a separate building in the park about 50 m from the palace. They are modern, comfortable, and very quiet.

Only breakfast is served at the hotel, but there are several good restaurants within walking distance. The hotel is open all year and major credit cards are accepted. The price of double rooms with breakfast begins at 1,950 ATS and suites cost up to 5,800 ATS.

Excursions:

See Schloß Prielau, Schloß Haunsperg, and Schloß Fuschl.

HOTEL SCHLOSS MÖNCHSTEIN
A-5020 Salzburg Zentrum
Mönchsberg Park 26
Telephone: 0662/848555-0
Fax: 0662/848559

Schloß Mönchstein is an ivy-clad, turreted castle on the Mönchsberg mountain high above the roof tops of Salzburg's Old Town. It is embraced by a 70 acre park and is an unmistakably aristocratic hideaway only five minutes from the center of the Old Town.

The castle was built in 1358 for guests of the Prince Archbishop and was expanded in 1649. A few years later an observatory tower was added, and the castle was donated to the University of Salzburg to be used by "the learned professors" to rest in it "from their strenuous brainwork." In the 18th century both Mozart and Haydn performed here, but in the 19th century the castle became a hotel. It is now a truly luxurious five star hotel owned by Baroness von Mierka. There are only 17 guest rooms and suites, all graciously appointed and splendidly decorated with many antiques. The ambiance is one of prosperity and restrained elegance in which tradition and old-world charm go hand in hand with contemporary comfort. On arrival guests are welcomed with a bowl of fruit and champagne, and fresh flowers grace their rooms throughout the stay. Service is impeccable and unobtrusive, but guests who desire even more attention can have a butler assigned to them. The hotel's chauffeured Rolls Royce is always standing by, and a private helicopter pad in the park is also available.

The hotel's five-star main restaurant offers a great variety of dishes prepared to perfection and served with great elegance.

There is a tennis court on the hotel grounds and a golf course in the vicinity.

The hotel is clearly top of the line in every respect.

Double rooms including breakfast cost between 2,400 and 6,200 ATS depending on the room and the season. They are most expensive in late July and August during the Salzburg Festival. The hotel is open all year, and Visa, MasterCard, and Diners credit cards are honored.

Excursions:

Please see Schloß Prielau, Schloß Haunsperg and Schloß Fuschl.

SCHLOSS NEUHAUS
A-5023 Salzburg
Kühbergstraße 1
Telephone: 0662/643616
Fax: 0662/643616

The castle is in a superb location on a 498 m high wooded knoll on the fringes of the Kühberg mountain in an eastern suburb of Salzburg. Its existence was first recorded in 1219 but the castle was rebuilt in 1424 and again in 1851. It is named after Prince Archbishop Eberhard III von Neuhaus who made it his summer residence in 1424 because of the splendid view the castle affords of sunsets over Salzburg. The outside appearance of the building has not changed since 1851, but two of its towers were converted to suites in 1988. The hotel part of the castle now consists of three suites with a total of six beds. Each suite is luxuriously decorated in a different style. One is very modern, another is in the Biedermeier style, and the third in the Baroque style. All are spacious and have modern conveniences including kitchens. The castle is full of antiques and other collector's items and houses one of Salzburg's best art galleries. It also hosts chamber music concerts.

This castle hotel has a four-star rating but is in many respects so different from other hotels that rating it by the usually standards is very difficult.

The hotel is open all year and the price of a suite for two persons is 4,000 - 8,000 ATS. An additional 100 ATS per person is charged for breakfast. There is no restaurant but the hotel can make arrangements for an outside cook to prepare dinner in your kitchen and serve it in your own suite.

Excursions:
Please see Schloß Prielau, Schloß Haunsperg, and Schloß Fuschl.

HOTEL SCHLOSS FUSCHL
A-5332 Hof bei Salzburg
Telephone: 06229/22530
Fax: 06229/225353

Schloß Fuschl is 20 minutes east of Salzburg on Route 158. It is situated in a 40 acre park at the tip of a peninsula jutting into the dark blue Fuschlsee. Mountains surround this quiet lake and woods extend to its very edge.

The castle is a big, square, ivy-covered, tower-like edifice with a steeply pitched roof in whose center stands an unusually wide chimney. The building is painted yellow except for its window shutters, which are red and white striped, like those of most other old Austrian castles. Schloß Fuschl was built in 1450 as a hunting lodge and summer residence of the Prince Archbishops of Salzburg and was the site of lavish entertainment and spectacular hunts with packs of up to two hundred hounds. It reached the peak of its glory, pomp, and show in the first half of the 17th century after which its fortunes began to recede. It passed into private hands in 1833 and became a hotel in 1958. The present hotel complex comprises the castle and several adjoining buildings: the Gästehaus, the *Waldhaus*, the rustic *Jägerhaus*, and the modern bungalows on the beach. A spruce forest separates the *Jagdhof* (hunting lodge) from the other buildings. This lodge stands by itself on an elevation above the hotel golf course and offers gorgeous views of the golf course, the lake, the woods, and the surrounding mountains.

The main hall of the castle has a vaulted ceiling supported by stone columns, a large fireplace, oriental rugs on the parquet floor, and old oil paintings and hunting memos on its walls. There are several elegant dining rooms, but in good weather the sheltered terrace overlooking the lake is more appealing. The cuisine is outstanding and the service is first-rate.

There is a small beach and an exceptionally pretty marble indoor pool under a vaulted ceiling. Golf and tennis are available on the grounds. There is also a bowling alley, a rifle range, an exercise room, and a beauty center.

The guest rooms are large and airy. They are beautifully appointed with traditional furniture and have all the modern amenities. The suites are especially spacious and are sumptuously decorated with delicately inlayed antique furniture, oriental rugs, and oil paintings. Views from all the rooms that face the lake are superb. Schloß Fuschl is a hotel that stands out even among other hotels in the five-star category. It is a first class resort hotel in a magnificent setting run in the best tradition of great European hotels. It is open all year and major credit cards are honored.

Room prices vary from season to season. The price of double rooms ranges from 2,600 to 4,000 ATS including buffet breakfast. Half board costs an additional 490 ATS per person and is well worth taking.

Excursions:

A day trip through the Salzkammergut lake region begins on Route 158 in the direction away from Salzburg. When you reach St. Gilgen, an old summer resort on St. Wolfgangsee, make a left turn onto Route 154. A few kilometers down the road on the right side is Schloß Hüttenstein, a romantic little castle on a hill above a small lake. As soon as you reach Mondsee, take the road on the right along the lake to Unterach on Attersee (lake). In Unterach take Route 152 around the southern end of the lake and continue on it to Steinbach, where you turn right toward Gmunden. Gmunden is an old Upper Austrian town at the northern end of Traunsee, the second largest lake in the area. You can stroll there on the lakeside promenade from where there are scenic views of the lake, with the charming Schloß Orth on a small island just offshore

Schloß Orth

and high mountains in the distance. On the way back to Fuschl take Route 145 south along the west shore of Traunsee, through Traunkirchen (see Upper Austria) and the town of Ebensee, and continue on the same road along the picturesque Traun River to Bad Ischl. This is a major spa with numerous tourist attractions and a pâtisserie, Konditorei Zauner, whose fame in Austria is second only to that of Vienna's pâtisserie Demel. From there take Route 158 along St. Wolfgangsee back to the hotel.

For other excursions please see the chapters on Schloß Prielau, Schloß Haunsperg, and Landhaus Hubertushof (Styria).

KÄRNTEN
(CARINTHIA)

Wörther See

Carinthia is Austria's southernmost province. It has a population of about 545,000 and a surface area of 9,533 sq. km. It consists of a central basin with plains, low mountains, and many lakes surrounded by high mountain ranges that shelter the central basin from cold winds. As Mediterranean high pressure zones often encompass Carinthia, there are more sunny days here than anywhere else in Austria, and the temperature is noticeably warmer. The more than 200 lakes in the province are quite warm, some of them may even reach 28° C (about 82°F), which suggests that they might be fed by thermal springs. The province borders on Salzburger Land to the north, Styria to the north and east, Slovenia and Italy to the south, and East Tirol to the west.

It is a land of great beauty with rearing mountains and plunging valleys, flower-speckled alpine meadows, tranquil villages with onion-domed churches, and numerous wayside chapels and crosses. It has many castles and ruins but is still relatively devoid of tourists. Visitors usually come by road. The A-2 autobahn links Klagenfurt, the capital, with Graz (143 km) and Vienna (338 km) while the A-10 autobahn connects the province with Salzburg. The best road from Italy is the expressway from Udine to Villach, and the most picturesque road to Carinthia is Route 111 from East Tirol. It winds its way through the remote Lesachtal (valley) at the foot of the Dolomites, a limestone mountain range in which erosion has carved slender pinnacles and saw-edged ridges. The most spectacular approach, however, is the one from the province of Salzburg over the Großglockner Hochalpenstraße (see Schloß Prielau) to the charming high alpine village of Heiligenblut.

The highest mountain in Carinthia and the whole country is the 3,797 m high Großglockner, and the largest lake in the province is the 16 km long Wörther See.

Klagenfurt, the capital of Carinthia, has a population of 90,000. It was founded in the year 1161 in a swamp allegedly inhabited by a ferocious dragon, which is still the emblem of the city. A huge sculpture of the dragon is the centerpiece of the Dragon Fountain built in 1590 in the center of the Neuer Platz (New Square). The head of the dragon was modeled after the skull of a big animal, probably an ice age rhinoceros, found in a nearby swamp and now displayed in the Provincial Museum. The city became capital of the province in 1518 when the previous capital, St. Veit, incurred the wrath of Emperor Maximilian I by refusing accommodations to soldiers he had sent there to suppress a peasant uprising. The town is near the eastern end of Wörther See to which it is linked by a canal constructed in the 16th century to supply water to the city's moat. The center of the city is the Neuer Platz dominated by the Dragon Fountain and the Neues Rathaus (New Town Hall) built in 1580. A short distance north is the Alter Platz, center of the Old Town, that looks more like a wide street than a square. It is lined with handsome, mostly Baroque buildings and small shops. The square is in a traffic-free zone and is perfect for strolling and window shopping. On its west side is the 16th century Landhaus (Provincial Government Building). In its Großer Wappensaal (Great Heraldic Hall) hang 655 coats of arms of Corinthian nobles and in the Kleiner Wappensaal (Small Heraldic Hall), 298 more.

Tourist information is available at the Tourist Office in the Rathaus (Town Hall), Telephone: 0463/537223.

Carinthia

HOTEL SCHLOSS SEEFELS
A-9210 Pörtschach
Töschling 1
Telephone: 04272/2377
Fax: 04272/3704

    Schloß Seefels is about 15 km west of Klagenfurt, a short distance from the Pörtschach exit of the A-2 autobahn. The castle, as its name suggests, is on a ledge (*Fels*) by a lake (Wörther See), in a park which shields it from the hubbub of Pörtschach, a popular summer resort. Unfortunately, it is not an old historic castle but one built only in the 19th century as summer residence of a castle buff. It was much expanded about 25 years ago and was turned into a hotel. The hotel has 73 rooms and suites, the best of which are in the tower. All guest rooms are spacious and comfortably furnished, but rooms in the main building are prettier, more elegant, and have better views than rooms in the new wing. Rooms facing the lake have balconies with views of the large shimmering lake, the village of Maria Wörth on the opposite shore, and the far off Karawanken mountain range. The hotel's fashionable dining room is exceptionally bright and airy as its roof and the wall facing the lake are made of glass. There is an indoor-outdoor swimming pool, a fitness and a beauty center, and six tennis courts. A few steps from the hotel is a large pier for sunbathing and swimming. Sailboats and motorboats dock there, and excursion boats pick up hotel guests for trips to Klagenfurt, Velden, and Maria Wörth. The hotel is open from April through October and major credit cards are accepted. The price of double rooms in this five-star hotel is 2,780 - 4,780 ATS including buffet breakfast and a five course dinner. In early September, when the weather is usually perfect and the water still quite warm, the highest price drops from 4,780 ATS to 3,380 ATS.

Excursions:

- Wörther See is 16 km long, up to 1.5 km wide, and up to 84 m deep. It is clean and its temperature may reach 28°C (82°F). Boat tours make stops at the two prettiest lakeside towns: Maria Wörth and Velden. Maria Wörth (population 2,000) is almost directly across the lake from Pörtschach. It is a small and quiet resort whose photographs figure prominently in advertisements for Wörther See. There are two churches there, both old, one Romanesque and the other Gothic. The smaller Romanesque church goes back to the middle ages and has beautiful 12th century frescos and 15th century stained-glass windows. Velden is at the western end of the lake and is the most fashionable resort in the area, particularly popular with film stars, pop musicians, and other celebrities from the world of entertainment. There is a beautiful lakeside promenade and a lovely lakeside castle, Schloß Velden, a five-star hotel now closed for renovation.

- A very enjoyable day trip by car begins on the A-2 autobahn in the direction of Klagenfurt, where you pick up Route 83 toward St. Veit. About 20 km north of Klagenfurt, turn right onto Route 82, and soon you will see a giant castle on the right side of the road. Burg Hochosterwitz is perched on a steep, 139 m high cliff, which rises precipitously out of the plain. There has been a castle there since the year 860, but the present one was built in the 16th century for defense against the Turks. A narrow road hewn from the rock twists up the side of the mountain and passes through 14 successive fortifications, each of them seemingly impregnable, before reaching the main wall of the castle proper. No foe ever managed to get even that far, let alone to conquer the castle itself. Although the castle is privately owned, much of it is open to the public. Its chapel on the edge of the precipice contains the remains of members of the Khevenhüller

Hochosterwitz

family, who built the castle and still own it. From a point next to the chapel are sweeping views of the fertile plain deep below and of a big swath of southeastern Carinthia.

- On the way back, retrace your steps on Route 82 and continue on it for 7-8 km to St. Veit an der Glan, the original capital of Carinthia. Much of the town's high wall still stands while its wide moat is now a pretty lawn. There is an attractive square in the center of the city, and the 12th century parish church and 15th century Rathaus (Old Town Hall) deserve a visit.

- There are about 20 castles in the vicinity of St. Veit and those who want to continue this foray into medieval times would do well to drive a few kilometers northwest of the city to Burg Frauenstein, a graceful and well-preserved castle with six impressive towers.

- An excursion to the spectacular Raggaklamm (gorge) also called Raggaschlucht is a whole day trip which begins on the A-2 autobahn heading west toward the intersection with A-10. Take the A-10 autobahn north, and near Seeboden get onto Route 100. Follow this road to Lurnfeld where you pick up Route 106. The Town of Flattach is 27 km down the road, and just before it a sign points left to Raggaklamm, which is only 2 km from the road. At the parking lot, take the foot path through the gorge carved by the Ragga river, which here plunges over a series of eight wild waterfalls. The path crisscrosses the roaring stream over flimsy-looking wood bridges, while climbing all the time at a fairly steep angle. At a few points one can barely squeeze through the narrow space between the cold, wet rock and the wood rail which separates the hiker from the thundering torrent below. The walls of the gorge are so close to each other that they almost touch at the top, and at one point the path threads its way under a huge round boulder wedged between the two walls.

- On the way back to the hotel you can swim in the very large and warm Millstätter See, which is reached by driving south on Route 106 and then on Route 100 to Seeboden, from where you continue on Route 98 along the lake to Millstatt. The town allegedly derives its name from the Latin *mille statuae* (thousand statues). A very devout early Christian prince is said to have found here a pagan temple with a thousand statues. He destroyed them all. To commemorate his deed a church was built and the prince's body buried under the altar. Several centuries later, when a priest who had taken a dim view of the prince refused to conduct the traditional annual service in his memory, the whole church except for the altar with the prince's remains, sank and remains to this day about 1 meter below the level of the surrounding ground. There is also a historic former Benedictine Abbey in Millstatt. It was founded in 1070 and in one of its arcaded courtyards stands a linden tree thought to be 1,000 years old.

HOTEL SCHLOSS LEONSTAIN
A-9210 Pörtschach
Hauptstraße 228
Telephone: 04272/28160
Fax: 04272/2823

Schloß Leonstain is in Pörtschach, a town on Wörther See, about 12 km from Klagenfurt and only a few kilometers from the A-2 autobahn. A record from the year 1166 mentions a fortified castle by the same name on a nearby hill. According to a legend, one of its owners had a tragic love affair with a mermaid in the lake. About 500 years ago the uncomfortable fortress-like castle was abandoned, and the present more comfortable castle was built by the lake. In 1645 the castle became property of the Jesuits and later of the Benedictine Order. Here, Johannes Brahms spent the summer months of 1877 and 1878, and here he composed his second symphony and violin concerto. At the beginning of this century, the castle was acquired by its present owners, the family Neuscheller, and was turned into a hotel in 1950. Giant copper beech, chestnut, and linden trees, pretty lawns and shady courtyards are part of this quaint and romantic castle whose white walls are covered with grapevine and ivy. During renovation its old architecture was painstakingly preserved while modern amenities were tastefully incorporated. The castle now successfully blends contemporary standards of comfort with the dignity of a former age. The hotel's public rooms are most attractive. Its elegant restaurant deservedly enjoys an excellent reputation and attracts many outside guests.

Across the street are the hotel's private swimming, sailing, wind surfing, and water skiing facilities. Tennis and golfing are also available.

This four-star castle hotel has a great deal of charm and character. It is open from May through October and has 35 bedrooms and 10 suites. Double rooms cost 2,300 - 3,020 ATS, and the price includes half board with a four course dinner. American Express, Visa, and Diners cards are accepted.

Excursions:
See Schloß Seefels.

HOTEL SCHLOSS MOOSBURG
A-9062 Moosburg
Telephone: 04272/83206
Fax: 04272/83206-23

The small village of Moosburg is west of Klagenfurt and only 6-7 km from Pörtschach and the Wörther See. It is reached from Pörtschach by a scenic road that runs through woods and pastures, past a few small lakes.

The castle is in its own park on a knoll next to one of the lakes. It was built by Leonhard von Ernau at the beginning of the 16th century when his nearby old castle became uninhabitable. Significant alterations were made in the early part of the 17th century at which time a chapel was also added. During the Counter Reformation in the 17th century, the Protestant von Ernaus refused to convert to the Catholic faith. The family was expelled from Austria and the castle and estates were taken over first by the von Ehrenthal family and then by the Counts Kronegg. The Counts Goess, the castle's present owners, acquired the property in 1708 and had it converted into a hotel in 1993.

Schloß Moosburg is a massive rectangular stone and stucco structure apparently built in two parts. One has three and the other four stories, but both parts are equally high. The castle roof is steeply pitched adding even more height to this towering building. A wall with small towers surrounds much of the castle. Above its main gate, carved in stone, are the coats of arms of the Counts Kronegg-Zinzendorf. The most memorable feature inside the castle is its large Gothic Knights' Hall, whose ceiling is supported by four octagonal stone columns. Portraits of ancestors and other aristocrats adorn the walls of several public rooms. There are 15 bedrooms and 2 suites tastefully furnished in a combination of the traditional and rustic styles. Baths and toilets are modern and are in separate rooms. There is a restaurant in the castle and an indoor swimming pool, while a lakeside beach and two tennis courts are in the park.

The hotel takes great pride in its nearby golf course and the beauty center. The hotel has a four-star rating and is open from April through October. The price of a double room with buffet breakfast is 1,500 - 2,200 ATS. Major credit cards are honored.

Excursions:

See Schloß Seefels.

SCHLOSS HALLEGG
A-9061 Klagenfurt-Wölfnitz
Krumpendorf
Telephone: 0463/49311-0
Fax: 0463/49311-8

The castle is 1.5 km north of the lakeside resort of Krumpendorf and 7 km west of Klagenfurt, from where it is reached by the A-2 autobahn to Krumpendorf and then a well-marked road to Hallegg.

This spectacular fortress-like, picture perfect medieval castle will elate all castle enthusiasts. The property belonged to the von Hallegg family as early as 1198, but the present castle was built between 1213 and 1570. It stands proudly on a hill and overlooks a vast expanse of fields and woods. Behind it is a park with many big old trees, a secluded small lake with bathing facilities and a tennis court. The castle is approached by a gravel drive leading through the park to a huge fortified gate above which the von Hallegg crest is carved in stone. The thick wood and steel gate opens onto a beautiful arcaded courtyard. The public rooms in the hotel are spacious, with vaulted ceilings, parquet floors and oriental rugs, and their walls are hung with old arms and hunting trophies. The most impressive chamber in the castle is the immense 16th century Knights' Hall.

The hotel has 15 large, nicely furnished guest rooms with modern amenities, but there is no restaurant. Only breakfast is offered and, weather permitting, it is served under the arcades on top of the castle wall. From here are superb views of fields on the one side and of the courtyard decked with flowers on the other.

This three-star hotel is open from May to the end of September. Double rooms cost 900 - 1,040 ATS including buffet breakfast. No credit cards are accepted.

Excursions:

See Schloß Seefels.

HOTEL SCHLOSS ST. GEORGEN
A-9020 Klagenfurt
Sandhofweg 8
Telephone: 0463/468490
Fax: 0463/4684970

Schloß St. Georgen is located in its own park only 3 kilometers north of the center of Klagenfurt. It is rather close to the airport, but fortunately no flights arrive or depart from it at night.

The church of St. George attached to the castle is known to have stood there in 1216, but the existence of the castle was not recorded until 1574, when it was owned by Hans von Hauß. It was redesigned and enlarged in the 17th century and was severely damaged at the end of World War II. During its restoration after the war, graves of Knights of the Teutonic Order were found under the chapel floor, suggesting that the Order may at one time have owned the property.

The castle is now a charming small hotel. It is entered through an impressive white entrance hall with a vaulted ceiling and a black and white marble floor. The hall is furnished with comfortable arm chairs and a few antique pieces, and its walls are decorated with hunting trophies. The castle chapel is open to visitors, and in its first pew is an eerie life-sized figure of a monk kneeling in prayer.

The hotel has 16 large and well-appointed bedrooms with neat bathrooms. Each room is decorated in a different style, and in some rooms the walls and the vaulted ceilings are painted with romantic landscapes. Most rooms look out on the castle's leafy park.

The hotel has a four-star rating and is open all year. The price of double rooms varies from 1,500 to 1,700 ATS and includes buffet breakfast. No other meals are offered. All major credit cards are welcomed.

Excursions:
See Schloß Seefels.

STEIERMARK
(STYRIA)

Steiermark is the second largest Austrian province. It is 16,387 sq. km large and has a population of about 1,185,000. It is bounded by Upper and Lower Austria on the north, Burgenland on the east, Slovenia on the south, and Carinthia and Salzburger Land on the west. The province is mostly mountainous, but in its eastern half high mountains gradually give way to gently rolling hills. This heavily forested land is rich in game. There are *Gams* (mountain goats) in the higher elevations, and R*eh* and *Hirsch* (kinds of deer) in the lower, where also wild boars and bears are occasionally seen. Forestry and pastoral farming support the population of the northern part of the province, but fruit growing and wine production are very important in the lower regions of eastern and southern Styria. Despite some iron mining, Styria remains a quaint agricultural province of great natural beauty. It has largely eschewed industrialization and has so far also escaped the onslaught of mass tourism. There are only a couple of ski resorts of international renown and, except for the lakes in the Salzkammergut area, there are hardly any famous summer resorts either. The unspoiled beauty of Styria can, therefore, still be enjoyed at a leisurely pace and at a cost much more affordable than in the heavily promoted provinces of Salzburg and Tirol. That is why Austrians, well-known for their appreciation of quiet homey comfort (*gemütlichkeit*), tend to spend their vacations in Styria, often referred to as the green heart of Austria.

Graz is the capital of Styria and with a population of about 245,000 is Austria's second largest city. It derives its name from the Slovene word *gradec* (little castle), and lies on the banks of the Mur, the largest river in the province. It is a major industrial, commercial, and cultural center with a university, a medical school, a technical college, an academy of music and drama, and an opera. The city is dominated by the 473 m high Schloßberg, a hill on which once stood a mighty fortress demolished in 1809 under the peace treaty with Napoleon. Only its clock tower built in 1561 was spared and is now the city's principal landmark.

The Hauptplatz (Main Square) is the center of the Old Town. In it stands a statue of Archduke Johann (1782-1859), a Habsburg who lived in rural Styria among common people by whom he was adored. In the adjacent Herrengasse there are several lovely old buildings including the 17th century Landeszeughaus (arsenal), now a museum. It houses a collection of armor and old arms large enough to equip an army of almost 30,000 soldiers. On the opposite side of the street is a Gothic church in which Tintoretto's Ascension is the most notable painting. The Landesmuseum Joanneum, endowed by Archduke Johann, also deserves to be seen, and especially its Alte Galerie (Old Gallery) in which there are important paintings and sculptures. Northeast of the Hauptplatz stands what is left of the huge 15th century Burg (castle), and near it is the Dom (cathedral),from the same century.

The top of the Schloßberg is best reached by funicular. The mountain overlooks the Old Town and affords panoramic views of the city and its surroundings. A gravel path through the large park brings one down to the very attractive Opera House.

Graz can be reached by plane, by train (2.5 hours from Vienna), or by car. Autobahns A-2 and A-9 intersect just south of the city. They connect Graz with Vienna (205 km), Klagenfurt (143 km), northern Austria, and Slovenia.

The Tourist Office at Herrengasse 16, Telephone: 0316/835241, will provide information and make room reservations in the whole province.

LANDHAUS HUBERTUSHOF
A-8992 Altaussee
Puchen 86
Telephone: 03622/71280
Fax: 03622/71280-80

This charming small hotel is in the northwest corner of Styria, about 90 km east of Salzburg, from where it is reached by Route 158, past Fuschlsee and St. Wolfgangsee to Bad Ischl. In Bad Ischl, turn right onto Route 145 to Bad Aussee, then follow signs to Altaussee, only 4.5 km away.

Hubertushof is on a sunny hill overlooking the village and the pretty Altaussee Lake. It was originally the hunting lodge of a prince and is still owned by a member of the family. Its present owner, the Countess Strasoldo-Graffemberg, born Princess Oettingen-Wallerstein, turned the lodge into a hotel about 20 years ago but has succeeded in preserving in it the ambiance of a prosperous and comfortable Austrian country house. Many walls in the building are panelled while others are painted white and sport a great number of various hunting trophies. The furniture, much of it antique, ranges in style from alpine to Biedermeier. As the Countess, an amiable, matronly old lady dressed in *Dirndl* (regional costume), believes that a restaurant in the house would adversely impact the homey ambiance she is striving to preserve, only breakfast is offered. It is served in a charming panelled room or, weather permitting, on a balcony from where there are fine views of the lake.

In this three-star hotel, double rooms with bathroom and balcony cost 1,200 - 1,300 ATS, including buffet breakfast. Major credit cards are accepted.

The hotel is open for a few days around Christmas and Easter, and from the middle of May through the middle of October.

Excursions:

A short car ride on a toll road brings one to the top of the 1,830 m Loser, which towers over the Altaussee and offers magnificent views of the lake and the snow-capped 2,995 m high Hoher Dachstein.

Hallstatt

- For a pleasant day trip closer to the Dachstein, take the road from Altaussee to Bad Aussee, and from there the fairly steep road to Hallstatt, a town in Upper Austria that definitely deserves to be explored. It is best to leave the car in the parking lot by the road high above Hallstatt and to proceed on foot down the narrow streets of this ancient small town crowded on a strip of land between the dark blue waters of the Hallstätter See and the steeply rising mountain behind it. In the center of the town is a small cobbled square enclosed by charming little houses painted in pastel colors with shops on the ground floor and windows and balconies overflowing with brightly colored flowers. The sides of many houses are completely covered by amazingly well-espaliered pear trees.

• Continue from Hallstatt along the lake to Route 166, which should be followed till Gosau. A smaller road on the left leads from Gosau to Gosausee (lake) about 7 km away. Actually, there are three Gosau lakes; the one you have reached is the Vorderer Gosausee. From its lakeside restaurant there is a wonderful view of the turquoise lake against the backdrop of the gray rock and white snow of the Dachstein. A path will take you to the middle and the highest of the Gosau lakes, and on to the glaciers. The highest lake is about one and one half hours from the parking lot.

• A short car trip to Grundlsee and Toplitzsee begins with a left turn in Bad Aussee onto the well-marked road to Grundlsee. Continue along the picturesque lake through the village of Grundlsee to Gößl, then walk about 2 km through woods to the much smaller Toplitzsee. A short but fairly steep climb brings you from this lake to the even smaller Kammersee and the waterfall at the source of the Traun river.

HOTEL SCHLOSS PICHLARN
A-8952 Irdning
Gatschen 28
Telephone: 03682/22841-0
Fax: 03682/22841-6

The village of Irdning is in northern Styria in the valley of the river Enns at the junctions of Routes 145 and 146. The castle is a short distance east of the village on the side of a hill at the foot of the Tauern Mountains in a bucolic setting of fields and woods.

The history of the castle goes back to the year 1074, but most of the present castle was erected by the von Stainach family in the 16th and 17th centuries. The castle changed hands several times and became a hotel in 1969. Since 1989 it has belonged to Dr. Erich Kaub, who turned it into a resort hotel with an exceptionally pretty 18 hole golf course and made it a renowned equestrian center, complete with a riding hall and a paddock. There are also indoor and outdoor tennis courts, indoor and outdoor swimming pools, and a fitness center. The castle with its additions is a very large white building with several towers and a beautiful, wrought iron gate, behind which is a park with gravel paths and a huge linden tree at the hotel entrance.

There are 77 gracefully appointed rooms with all the modern conveniences and balconies with beautiful views of the peaceful countryside. The public rooms are spacious, well-designed and elegant, and the two restaurants are attractive, especially the one decorated in the rustic style. This five-star hotel open all year is ideally suited for golfers and equestrians. Double rooms with half board cost 3,000 - 3,600 ATS in July and August, and somewhat less at other times. All major credit cards are honored.

Excursions:

For excursions in summer please see Landhaus Hubertushof. In winter, there is excellent skiing at Schladming, the site of international ski championships. Schladming is only 38 km west of Irdning on Route 146.

Styria

HOTEL SCHLOSS GABELHOFEN
A-8752 Wasendorf
Schloßgasse 54
Telephone: 03177/2212-0
Fax: 03177/2212-6

The hotel is on the right bank of the small Pöls river, just off Route S-36, a few kilometers north of Judenburg. It is 85 km from Graz and 210 km from Vienna.

Building of the castle began in 1490, but most of it was built only between 1536 and 1596, when the castle belonged to the Gabelhofer family. It has changed hands many times since 1775 and was turned into a hotel in 1994.

The castle is a large Renaissance structure with a wide moat which is now dry. It also has a thick wall with four defensive towers. The castle complex is entered over a bridge that used to be a drawbridge, behind which is a fortified gate. The castle proper is a large edifice dominated by a square tower. Its arcaded inner courtyard has been converted into a light and spacious lobby under a glass roof. The lobby is very modern but is nevertheless in perfect harmony with the rest of the old castle. There is also a second, more traditional and very attractive hall on the upper level. Ceilings in the restaurant, the barroom, and the large conference rooms are vaulted and supported by carved stone columns. Old oil paintings grace the walls of most public rooms. The hotel has 14 single and 40 double rooms, 2 suites and 1 junior suite. They are obviously new, spacious, and comfortable. Toilets and baths are in separate rooms.

The hotel is open all year and has a four-star rating. Double rooms with breakfast cost 1,610 ATS, and half board with dinner in the very chic restaurant costs an additional 260 ATS per person. All major credit cards are accepted.

Styria

BURGHOTEL DEUTSCHLANDSBERG
A-8530 Deutschlandsberg
Burgstraße 19
Telephone: 03462/5656
Fax: 03462/5656-22

This castle hotel is near the town of Deutschlandsberg, about 40 km south of Graz and only a couple of kilometers from Route 76. It was built in 1153 by a Prince Archbishop of Salzburg and has changed hands many times. Through most of the 19th century it belonged to the Prince of Liechtenstein but became town property in 1932. It is now again privately owned and has been a hotel since 1989.

The castle sits on the side of a hill overlooking lush woods, meadows, and a large expanse of vineyards. It is in the center of a wine-producing area often referred to as the Styrian Paradise. The hotel consists of a large yellow main building dating from 1548, flanked on one side by a small tower and on the other by a big stone tower and the ruins of the original castle. The main tower is 25 m high, and its walls are 2 m thick at the base. The former Knights' Hall, now an attractive restaurant, is in an adjoining building.

There are 25 comfortably appointed guest rooms in this four-star hotel. Double rooms with half board cost 1,220 ATS.

The hotel is open from the beginning of April through the month of December. No credit cards are accepted.

Excursions:

Schloß Frauenthal is only 3 km away and offers excellent golfing and horseback riding. Guests staying at Burg Deutschlandsberg are welcomed.

SCHLOSS KAPFENSTEIN
A-8353 Kapfenstein
Telephone: 03157/2202
Fax: 03157/2202-4

Schloß Kapfenstein is a very old fortified castle about 60 km southeast of Graz and 12 km from the Slovenian border. It was built in the 12th century on a 450 m high basalt mountain amidst the rolling hills of southeastern Styria, where it is surrounded by small forests, farmland, and vineyards. It was destroyed by the Hungarians in 1238 and rebuilt mostly in the 16th and 17th centuries. The castle and the surrounding vineyards have been owned by the Winkler-von Hermaden family since 1898 and are now run as a successful wine business and a small hotel.

A steeply climbing, winding road brings one through a narrow gate into the courtyard at the hotel entrance. The castle has 7 very attractive, tastefully furnished, comfortable, and very quiet double rooms with stunning views. All rooms have modern bathrooms. The dining room is elegantly decorated in the Austrian rustic style very much in keeping with the ambiance of an old castle. The breakfast room is equally attractive, and the large terrace presents a panoramic view of the countryside all the way to the border. The hotel justifiably prides itself on the quality of its food and wine and the outstanding service and personal attention given to its guests.

Double rooms in this four-star hotel cost 1,900 ATS including buffet breakfast and a four course gourmet dinner. No credit cards are accepted.

Excursions:

A map of trails for walks through the peaceful countryside can be obtained at the hotel as can also a map for trips to other castles in the area. Castles Riegersburg, Kornberg, Herberstein, and Schielleiten are particularly interesting.

SCHLOSSHOTEL OBERMAYERHOFEN
A-8272 Sebersdorf
Telephone: 03333/2503-0
Fax: 03333/2503-50

The hotel is only a couple of kilometers from the Waltersdorf-Sebersdorf exit from the A-2 autobahn that connects Vienna and Graz. It is 124 km from Vienna and 55 km from Graz.

The castle is named after Bishop Heinrich Mayerhofer who owned it in the early part of the 14th century. In 1377 it became the property of the von Teuffenbach family and remained theirs for 230 years, but since 1777 the castle has been in the hands of the Counts Kottulinsky. The castle was so severely damaged at the end World War II that it took 30 years to restore it to its original condition. It became a hotel in 1986 and is presently managed by the Countess. The castle stands on elevated ground at the end of a long straight, partly cobbled drive. The complex is entered through a large gatehouse followed by a second gate through which one enters a beautiful arcaded central courtyard with a small lawn and balustrades heavy with flowers. Bedrooms are spacious, sumptuously decorated with period furniture, and have large windows with lovely views of the park and the fields. The marble bathrooms are large and modern, with huge triangular bathtubs and floor heating. The public rooms are furnished with antiques, and embellished with ornate tiled stoves, oriental rugs, frescos, and Gobelins. There is also a surprisingly large old chapel on the ground floor. The hotel's outstanding Goldesel Restaurant is in a separate building along the drive between the castle's two gates. This luxurious castle hotel has a four-star rating, but why the fifth star was withheld is a puzzle. There are 19 bedrooms and suites. Double rooms with breakfast cost 1,420 - 2,800 ATS. The hotel is open from March through December, and all major credit cards are honored.

Excursions:
　　Sightseeing trips to the castles listed under Schloß Kapfenstein are recommended.

BURGENLAND

With a population of only about 270,000 and a surface area of 396,000 sq. km., Burgenland is the smallest province of Austria except for the recently created province of Vienna. It is a narrow strip of land that borders on Slovakia and Hungary to the east, Slovenia to the south, and Lower Austria and Styria to the west. In it the eastern foothills of the Alps flatten and gradually dissolve into the great Pannonian Plain of Hungary. Burgenland is a rich agricultural area with forests covering the tops of its rounded hills, vineyards covering their sides, and fields of wheat, corn, and sunflowers covering the fertile plains. About 1/3 of Austrian wine is produced here as are most vegetables consumed in the nearby Vienna. The central feature of the province is the Neusiedler See, a part of which is in Hungary. The lake is 35 km long and up to 15 km wide but not more than 2 m deep and is therefore quite warm in summer. It is fringed with reeds in which nest more than 250 species of birds. The pretty town of Rust on its shore attracts a large number of visitors who come between May and late August to swim in the lake and to watch the storks that nest on many chimneys.

The population of the province is mostly of Germanic extraction but there are considerable Croatian and Hungarian minorities whose influence shows especially in the music, the dances, and the cuisine of Burgenland.

Eisenstadt, the capital of the province, is a small town of only about 11,000 inhabitants. It is approximately 50 km southeast of Vienna by Route 16, but parts of the new A-3 autobahn are already open to traffic and should be used whenever possible.

The town is dominated by the large park and the Baroque palace of the Princes Esterházy which at the time of its greatest glory had 200 rooms, including six glittering ball rooms. Most of the palace is now open to the public and is used for exhibitions and concerts. Especially pretty is the Haydn Room decorated with colorful frescos. It is here that Franz Joseph Haydn (1732-1809) performed many of his compositions for the first time, as he spent 30 years of his very productive life at the Palace as court composer and conductor. He is buried less than 1 km west of the palace in a mausoleum built by the Esterházys in 1932. The mausoleum is open to the public.

111

Burgenland

Information on the whole province can be obtained at the Burgenland Tourist Office, Schloß Esterházy, A-7000 Eisenstadt, Telephone: 02682/3384.

Information on the town is available at the Eisenstadt Tourist Office, A-7000 Eisenstadt, Hauptstraße 35, Telephone: 02682/2710.

HOTEL BURG BERNSTEIN
A-7434 Bernstein
Telephone: 03354/6382
Fax: 03354/6520

To reach the castle from Vienna (120 km), take the A-2 autobahn to the Krumbach exit. Continue on Route 55 through Krumbach to the outskirts of Kirchschlag, where you turn right onto the road to Bernstein, about 11 km away. In the center of the village of Bernstein turn right onto the castle drive lined with big old chestnut trees. It leads up a 619 m high knoll to the huge, old, fortified castle whose 36 m high tower is visible from afar. Its foundation dates from the Roman times, but the recorded history of the castle goes back only to the 12th century. It was expanded in the 14th, 15th, and 16th centuries but was almost completely destroyed in 1617 when lightening struck its gun powder house. It was rebuilt and enlarged to its present size in the 17th and 18th centuries.

The castle is entered through a massive gatehouse and an outer courtyard, from where one proceeds on foot through a big fortified gate into the large inner courtyard. In the entrance hall is a majestic old stone stairway that leads up to the guest rooms. It is decorated with crests of the castle's previous owners. The guest rooms and suites are enormous and are entirely furnished with antiques. They have wood floors, oriental rugs, and big ornate stoves that are fed from the corridors. Bathrooms are well appointed and modern. There is a beautiful chapel inside the castle, where services are held on holy days. The largest and most impressive room in the castle is the huge, white Knights' Hall with

113

Baroque plaster work on its ceiling and around the deeply recessed windows. The Hall is now a charming restaurant where dinner is served by candlelight.

Burg Bernstein is a genuine old hilltop castle in a romantic setting of hills, woods, and fields, and it definitely continues to be more a castle than a hotel. It is a place to unwind, delve into the past, and meditate in complete quiet, undisturbed by traffic noise, television, radio, or telephone. Even the hotel business telephone is down in the village.

The hotel has 10 bedrooms, which cost 1,800 ATS. The price includes a buffet breakfast, but for an additional 290 ATS per person one can have half board whith an excellent three or four course candlelight dinner. Burg Bernstein has a three-star rating.

The hotel is open from May through the middle of October. Credit cards are accepted but are not exactly welcomed.

Excursions:

- There are several easy walking trails behind the castle through fields and woods which abound with deer. The castle manager will provide you a very detailed map on which the best trails are marked.

- We also recommend visits to other castles in the province, especially the mighty Burg Forchtenstein, whose walls are up to 7 m thick. It is reached by driving north on Route 50 to Route S-31. Near Mattersburg you will see signs pointing toward the castle, which is 5 or 6 km away.

- A day trip to Eisenstadt and Rust is also recommended. Eisenstadt is reached by driving north on Route 50. Both towns were briefly described earlier in this chapter.

BURG LOCKENHAUS
A-7442 Lockenhaus
Telephone: 02616/2394
Fax: 02616/2095

Lockenhaus is about 120 km south of Vienna and 15 km east of Bernstein. The castle is on a small, densely forested mountain and is accessible only by a long, tree-lined drive.

The older, upper part of the castle and its main tower were built in the early 13th century; and the newer, lower part, in the 17th century. Through its long history the castle has belonged to several, mostly Hungarian aristocratic families of whom the most recent owners (up to 1968) were the Princes Esterházy. It now belongs to a foundation and was converted into a hotel in the 1980's.

There are several attractive courtyards in the castle, a chapel with 13th century frescos, and a beautiful Gothic Knights' Hall. It has a high vaulted ceiling supported by stone columns.

There are 7 bedrooms in the castle and 27 suites for 2 - 4 persons in an adjoining building. The suites are equippped with telephones, cable TV, and modern kitchens. The rooms in the castle proper are of good size and are tastefully furnished with period furniture including some antiques. They offer fine views of forests and a small lake.

The castle houses a museum and in summer is the site of chamber music concerts. There is also a rustic tavern in the castle in which hearty meals are served in medieval proportions.

This three-star hotel is open from the middle of January through the middle of December. Double rooms costs 700 - 900 ATS and half and full board are also available. No credit cards are accepted.

Excursions:
Same as from Burg Bernstein.

OBERÖSTERREICH
(Upper Austria)

The province of Upper Austria extends from the Czech border in the north to the provinces of Salzburg and Styria in the south, and from Bavaria (Germany) in the west to Lower Austria in the east. It encompasses an area of 11,980 sq. km. and has a population of about 1,300,000. The Danube bisects this province, and it is the part of the province south of the Danube that is of greatest interest to tourists. The Salzkammergut Lake district, most of which is in Upper Austria, is particularly attractive. Its large, clean lakes surrounded by towering mountains provide a breathtaking scenery, one of the finest in Europe. The largest of the lakes is Attersee, which is 20 km long and up to 3 km wide. It is at the foot of the Höllen-Gebirge (mountain range), which separates it from the somewhat smaller but prettier Traunsee. There are stunning views of Traunsee from the lakeside promenade in the town of Gmunden (see page 81) and also from a wooded promontory in the village of Traunkirchen, about halfway down the west shore of the lake. South of Traunsee is the Hallstätter See surrounded by mountains, the highest of which is the 2,995 m Dachstein. The small, old town of Hallstatt (see page 100) was described in the section on Landhaus Hubertushof, Styria.

The water temperature of most Salzkammergut Lakes ranges between refreshing and chilling, but the temperature of Mondsee may reach 26°C (79°F) and it is, therefore, the favorite lake of families with small children. The scenic St. Wolfgangsee is also fairly warm. Most of it is in the province of Salzburg, but the town of St. Wolfgang is in Upper Austria. This very old town, its pilgrimage church, and the quaint hotel Weisses Rössl attract crowds of sightseers and are best visited before or after the main season.

Linz, the capital of Upper Austria has a population of 200,000 and is the third largest city in the country. Its center is the mostly Baroque Hauptplatz (main square) faced by the 17th century Rathaus (Town Hall). North of it is the Nibelungenbrücke, the main bridge across the Danube, and south of the square is the shopping district, whose hub is the Landstraße lined with boutiques and upscale stores. West of the square, on a hill above the Danube, is the Linzer Schloß, where Emperor Friedrich III resided in the 15th century when Linz was briefly his capital. The palace was almost completely destroyed by fire in the 19th century but has been rebuilt and is now a museum. Also west of the square is the

Martinskirche, built in the 8th century and largely preserved in its original shape and style. Southwest of the main square on Klosterstraße is the Landhaus, built in the 16th century and rebuilt after a fire in the 19th century. It is now the seat of the Provincial Government, but was once a school where the famous astronomer Kepler taught in the 17th century.

Linz is an important center of industry and commerce. It has extensive port installations on the Danube, is an important railroad junction and is on the A-1 autobahn between Vienna (181 km) and Salzburg (130 km). It has an airport that connects it with other cities in Austria as well as with Frankfurt, Zurich, Paris, Amsterdam, and Milan.

Tourist information can be obtained at the Upper Austria Tourist Association, A-4010 Linz, Schillerstraße 50, Telephone: 0732/6630-21 and at the Linz Tourist Office A-4010 Linz, Hauptplatz 34, Telephone: 0732/2393-17-77.

SCHLOSS FEYREGG
A-4540 Bad Hall
Telephone: 07258/2591

Bad Hall is a small spa town not far from the A-1 autobahn connecting Vienna, Linz, and Salzburg. At the Sattledt exit take Route 122 through Kremsmünster, then follow the signs to Bad Hall, which is about 10 km from Kremsmünster. Schloß Feyregg is on the western outskirts of Bad Hall where the town borders on lush green farmland.

Mention is made of this estate in a 9th century record, but the castle was not built until the 12th century. It was enlarged in the 15th and was completely redesigned in the 18th century, when all traces of its medieval past were buried under Baroque embellishments. It now gives the impression of a very well-preserved, lovingly maintained, modest and unpretentious Baroque castle. Its two towers and the main building are painted yellow and white and the whole castle is set in a small garden with statutes and a fountain.

Eleven guest rooms are located in a wing of the castle. They have recently been renovated, are immaculate, and have modern amenities. The public rooms are equally attractive. There is a nice old stone floor in the entrance hall and a lovely oriental rug in the cozy breakfast room. There is no restaurant at the castle, but there is one 600 m away.

This four-star hotel is open all year. The price of a double room with breakfast is 1,900 - 2,400 ATS. No credit cards are accepted.

Excursions:

- In the nearby town of Kremsmünster, halfway between Bad Hall and the A-1 autobahn, is a huge Benedictine Abbey founded in 777 by Tassilo III, Duke of Bavaria, to mark the grave of his young son Gunther, killed on that spot by a wild boar. The present church was built in the 13th century in the Early Gothic style but was subsequently remodeled in the Baroque style. The two most cherished possessions of the church are Gunther's carved sarcophagus and a priceless gilded copper chalice made in 765 for the wedding of Tassilo with the daughter of the King of the Longobards. It is delicately carved with the likenesses of Christ and the Evangelists, and engraved with a Latin inscription reading "Tassilo the Mighty Duke + Lintpric the Royal Maiden." The Abbey's library contains 100,000 volumes and 416 old manuscripts as well as a hand-written Bible from the year 800.

- The Salzkammergut Lakes are within easy driving range. They have been described earlier in this chapter and also under Schloß Fuschl (Salzburger Land) and Landhaus Hubertushof (Styria).

NIEDERÖSTERREICH
(Lower Austria)

The names of the neighboring provinces of Upper and Lower Austria do not refer to their elevation above sea level but to their position along the course of the Danube. Thus, Lower Austria is called "lower" because it is downstream from Upper Austria. Lower Austria, which is 19,171 sq. km. large and has a population of about 1,430,000, is the largest of the nine provinces of Austria. It extends from the Czech border in the north to Styria in the south and from Slovakia and Burgenland in the east to Upper Austria in the west. The Danube flows through it from west to east and divides it into a northern and a southern half. The plateau-like northern half is an extension of the Czech mountains while the southern half comprises the eastern foothills of the Alps including the 2,076 m high Schneeberg. The slopes along the Danube are terraced and covered with vineyards that produce 60% of the country's grape harvest and some of its best wines. Fortified castles crown the tops of many hills along the Danube, and there are 550 castles and castle ruins in this province. They were built because Lower Austria's location on the banks of the Danube put it on the route invaders from the east always took on their way to Central Europe. The province is the cradle of Austria and is the region that was being referred to wnen the word Austria was first used in the 10th century.

Even though Vienna is both historically and geographically the center of this province, administratively it no longer is part of it, as the city of Vienna has become a separate province.

St. Pölten, with a population of 51,000, is the capital of Lower Austria and its largest city. It is 66 km west of Vienna and 125 km east of Linz and is linked with both by the A-1 autobahn. It is an industrial town but has a number of handsome, mostly Baroque buildings huddled around four almost adjoining squares. The westernmost is the Rathausplatz (Town Hall Square), and the easternmost, not more than 750 m away, is the Domplatz (Cathedral Square). The cathedral was built in the 12th and 13th centuries in the Romanesque style, but like many other medieval churches throughout Austria was remodeled in the 18th century in the Baroque style. The adjacent Bishop's Palace was built in the 17th century on the site of a Benedictine monastery founded in the 8th century. Even though the center of the town is of interest and is not devoid of charm, there is little reason for vacationers to make a special detour to sightsee in St. Pölten as there are many other towns in Austria where their time and effort will be more richly rewarded.

Tourist information can be obtained at the Tourist Office in the Town Hall, A-3100 St. Polten, Rathausplatz 1, Telephone: 02742/3354.

SCHLOSS DROSENDORF
A-2095 Drosendorf an der Thaya
Schloßpaltz 1
Telephone: 2915/23210
Fax: 2915/232140

The medieval walled town of Drosendorf is in the extreme northern part of Lower Austria only 4 km from the Czech border. The town is on a knoll on the right bank of the Thaya River, which lazily meanders through fertile fields and lush forests. It is about 125 km northwest of Vienna from where it is reached by following Route 4 through Horn to Geras, and then Route 30 for 23 km to Drosendorf. A narrow street climbs up a hill to a cobbled square in the center of this charming old city. The castle is only one block from the square on the edge of a plateau high above the Thaya River. It was built around the year 1100 and was acquired by the Habsburgs in 1278. In 1694 it was severely damaged by a fire and was then rebuilt in its present shape except that its very high tower was for some reason razed in 1710. Since 1822, it has belonged to the Hoyas-Sprinzenstein family.

The castle is a very large Baroque edifice with a cobbled inner courtyard accentuated by a fountain. Its corridors are unusually wide and their walls are lined with big deer antlers. The huge bedrooms are furnished with solid old furniture and some antiques, but the bathrooms are contemporary.

This three star-hotel is open all year. There are 21 rooms and 2 suites all with bathrooms. Double rooms cost 680 - 720 ATS including breakfast. No credit cards are accepted.

SCHLOSSHOTEL ROSENAU
A-3924 Schloß Rosenau bei Zwettl
Schloß Rosenau 1
Telephone: 2822/8221
Fax: 2822/82218

Schloß Rosenau is about 7 km west of the town of Zwettl and about 150 km northwest of Vienna from where it is accessed by the A-1 autobahn. After leaving the A-1 at Melk and crossing the Danube, turn left onto Route 3 and after about 4 km, turn right onto Route 216 toward Würnsdorf. In Würnsdorf make a right turn onto Route 36 and stay on it until you reach Zwettl. In Zwettl, turn left in the direction of Weitra, and 3.5 km down the road you will see a sign pointing left toward Schloß Rosenau.

This originally Renaissance castle was built in 1590 by Baron Greiß and was in the 18th century rebuilt in the Baroque style by Count Schallenberg who turned it into an important center of freemasonry. The castle was subsequently owned by several other aristocratic families, but after it suffered severe damage by Soviet troops stationed there after World War II, Baron Lazarini-Zobelsberg sold it to the town of Zwettl. The castle has since been converted into a hotel and conference center.

This small Baroque castle with a tall clock tower, a courtyard, and a small park is nestled amidst fields, woods, and rolling hills in a peaceful setting far from major roads and railroads. The castle has a very formal hall adorned with attractive 18th century frescos, and an equally formal dining room used only on special occasions. Masonic symbols survive in several public rooms and many more in the castle's masonic museum.

There is also a small Baroque chapel in the castle and a cozy rustic restaurant. This three-star hotel features 17 bedrooms and 2 suites comfortably outfitted with modern furniture.

Double rooms with half board cost 1,240 - 1,440 ATS, and we have been informed that the whole castle may be rented at the price of 77,000 ATS a night.

Credit cards are not accepted.

BURG OBERRANNA
A-3622 Mühldorf
Telephone: 02713/8221
Fax: 02713/8366

The shortest way from Vienna to Mühldorf is by Route 3 up the left bank of the Danube to Spitz, which is halfway between Melk and Krems. The alternate and somewhat faster way to Spitz is the A-1 autobahn to Melk, where one crosses the Danube and continues on Route 3 down the left bank of the river to Spitz. Either way, once in Spitz, take Route 217 to Mühlsdorf, which is 6.5 km away. From there, follow the road up the mountainside to the castle.

At the very beginning of the 12th century Count Formbach built here a church dedicated to St. George and a castle to protect it. In the 14th century the property was inherited by the von Neidegg family, who in

126

the 16th century enlarged the castle and turned it into a veritable fortress. From the 17th century on, the property changed hands repeatedly until it was recently thoroughly renovated and turned into a hotel.

The castle sits on a steep hill, its only accessible side protected by two rows of deep, wide moats and two big stone walls with towers. The moats are now dry and grassy, inhabited by deer and a few wild boars. After crossing a bridge over the outer moat and passing through a big gate in the outer wall, one drives to a narrow stone bridge over the inner moat. This bridge is crossed on foot, and then one continues through the second gate behind which is a tunnel-like passage through a wing of the fortress. It leads into the central courtyard surrounded by tiered renaissance arcades. The castle's main tower is a big square structure with arched Renaissance windows that offer spectacular views. Under the 12th century church of St. George is a vaulted crypt with interesting carved stone columns. The spacious hotel lounge has an old wood ceiling, and its wide board floor is covered with oriental rugs. It is furnished with antiques among which a large inlaid table is the most valuable. The Knights' Hall, in which breakfast is served, is less ornate while the quaint tavern is refreshingly rustic.

The hotel offers double and single rooms and suites with a total of only 12 beds. The ample rooms are furnished with many antiques, while bathrooms are new and have all the modern amenities. Everything in this hotel is in perfect order and in excellent condition.

The hotel has a three-star rating. It is open from May to November. Double rooms cost 1,200 ATS, including buffet breakfast, but lunch and dinner are not served. They are available in the nearby village inns. American Express and Visa cards are welcomed.

Excursions:

See Schloß Dürnstein.

HOTEL SCHLOSS DÜRNSTEIN
A-3601 Dürnstein
Telephone: 02711/212
Fax: 02711/351

    The small historic town of Dürnstein is on the left bank of the Danube, in the Wachau region renowned for its excellent wine. It is best reached from Vienna (80 km) by the A-1 autobahn to St. Pölten and from there by Route S-33 to Krems. Immediately after crossing the Danube, take Route 3 west along the Danube to Dürnstein.

    The castle is a Renaissance edifice built in 1630 on a ledge above the Danube. Through most of its history it was the property of the Princes Starhenberg but now belongs to the family Thiery, who have converted it into a luxurious hotel that meets the highest standards of even the most demanding guests. Its rooms and suites are decorated in the Baroque, the Biedermeier or the Empire style and boast antique furniture, oriental rugs, and elaborately decorated tiled stoves. The bathrooms are modern, spacious, and luxurious. The dining room ambiance is one of subdued elegance, and the food served there is superbly prepared and attractively presented. The Austrian pastry and the local wine are outstanding. In good weather meals are also served on a terrace directly over the Danube from where there are gorgeous views, especially at sunset. A refreshing breeze from the river keeps one comfortable there even on the warmest days.

There is a nice outdoor and a beautiful new indoor pool. Tennis courts are ten minutes away on foot and there are several golf courses in the vicinity.

The hotel is open from March to November and well deserves its five stars. There are 38 rooms and suites. The price of a double room with half board is 2,400 - 3,000 ATS. Major credit cards are welcomed.

Excursions:

There are many castles and monasteries in the area. A list of them with directions and descriptions can be obtained free of charge from the receptionist. We especially recommend visits to the town of Krems and the abbey in Melk.

- Krems is 5 km east of Dürnstein on Route 3. Its location in the Wachau, the heart of Austria's most important wine region, has made it an important center of viticulture and wine trade. Its Old Town is entered on foot through the Steiner Tor, a gate built in 1480 and guarded by a tall, square, Baroque tower flanked by two older and smaller round towers. The gate opens onto the main street lined with immaculate old buildigs. The Rathaus (Town Hall) was built in 1453 and expanded in 1549. A 15th century church is opposite the Town Hall, and the oldest section of Krems with many Gothic buildings begins behind the Rathaus. One of the oldest buildings is the 13th century Gozzoburg, which has an arcaded courtyard decorated with coats of arms. The Pfarrkirche St. Veit is also of interest. It is medieval, was originally built in the Romanesque style, later remodeled in the Gothic style, and in the 17th century redecorated in the Baroque style. A couple hundred meters west from it is a museum in a former Dominican Church built in the 13th century in a combination of the Late Romanesque and Early Gothic styles.

- To reach the Benedictine Abbey in Melk, drive from Dürnstein 28 km west on Route 3, along the left bank of the Danube. After crossing the river at Melk, follow the signs pointing to the Benedictiner Stift (Abbey), which is visible from afar. It is a structure of colossal proportions on a rocky plateau that overlooks the Danube and dominates the town of Melk. A castle already stood here in the 10th century. Margrave Leopold II von Babenberg donated it and the adjoining church to the Benedictine Order in 1089, and both the Abbey and the fortifications were expanded in stages through the ensuing centuries. The gigantic complex, whose southern side alone measures 300 m in length, encompasses a large twin-towered church and seven courtyards. Its western side ends in a large terrace, which overlooks the Danube and presents superb views up and down the river. Inside, the Imperial Staircase leads to the Imperial Rooms and the 196 m long Imperial Corridor in which are displayed portraits of many Austrian emperors. This corridor leads to the Marble Hall, whose ceiling is covered with paintings depicting the triumph of wisdom over brute force and extoling the moderate ways chosen by the House of Habsburg. The Abbey's world-famous library contains 75,000 volumes and 1,800 manuscripts. It is richly decorated and its ceiling is covered with beautiful 18th century paintings. The Abbey's church dedicated to Saints Peter and Paul is reputedly the most beautiful Baroque church north of the Alps. Especially admired are its 64 m high cupola, built in 1712 - 1714, and its ceiling paintings from the same period.

SCHLOSS ERNEGG
A-3261 Steinakirchen am Forst
Telephone: 07488/214
Fax: 07488/6771

Schloß Ernegg is about 110 km west of Vienna from where it is reached by the A-1 autobahn. At the Ybbs exit, take Route 25 south to Wieselburg, then turn right onto a secondary road to Steinakirchen. The castle is on the left side, about 1.5 km from this road. It is on a hill surrounded by woods, fields, a small river and two golf courses.

The history of the castle is long and convoluted. Emperor Otto II donated the land to the church in 979. A castle is known to have stood here in the 12th century. It was subsequently acquired by the von Oedt family, who rebuilt and enlarged it to its present size in 1524. Their coat of arms can be found on the main tower. The coat of arms on the front porch is that of the Auersperg family, who have owned the castle and the large estate since 1656. The present owner is Countess Hilda Auersperg-Lee, who several years ago converted the castle into a hotel. A long winding drive through a forest leads up to the castle gate at which a gigantic linden tree stands guard. It is said to be 1,000 years old, allegedly the largest linden tree in Austria. It would take at least 5 or 6 people holding hands to encircle its massive trunk.

The castle is a large building with two towers, one of them part of the 14th century chapel. In the center of the castle complex is a lovely Renaissance arcaded courtyard whose tiers are decked with bright flowers and hung with many huge deer antlers. There are 20 spacious bedrooms, all individually decorated with mostly antique furniture and pretty tiled stoves. Most bedrooms have private bathrooms. The salon is a Baroque jewel. All its furniture is antique, old family portraits grace the walls, and a white, glazed tile stove decorated with delicate gold ornaments is an eyecatcher. The castle dining room is less formal. Its large, simple, rustic stove and many hunting trophies on the walls make the ambiance of this room relaxed and cozy.

The hotel is open from May through October and has a three star rating. Double rooms with baths cost 1,200 ATS including buffet breakfast. Visa, MasterCard, and Diners credit cards are honored.

Excursions:

In addition to the trips suggested under Schloß Dürnstein consider also a trip to Lunzer See.

- Drive from the hotel east to Purgstall and turn right onto Route 25. Stay on Route 25 for about 30 km. Then, just before the village of Lunz, turn left onto the road to Lunzer See, only a few kilometers away. The lake is warm and very peaceful. There is a public beach at its far side as well as a couple of hotels and restaurants.

HOTEL SCHLOSS WEIKERSDORF
A-2500 Baden bei Wien
Schloßgasse 9-11
Telephone: 02252/48301
Fax: 02252/48301-150

Baden bei Wien is about 30 km south of Vienna from where it is reached by driving on the A-2 autobahn to the Baden exit. It can also be reached by bus or tram from the center of Vienna. Baden has been a spa since Roman times, but it did not gain fame until the early part of the 19th century when it became the summer residence of the Imperial Court. It is now a pleasant, leafy and quiet spa town.

Schloß Weikersdorf is in the most elegant section of the town. Its name is a corruption of the name of its 1233 owner, Hugo von Weiherburg. The castle changed hands many times. In 1507 it became the property of Matthias Corvinus, King of Hungary, and later in the same century it was destroyed by the Turks during their first invasion of Austria. It was rebuilt only to be devastated again during the second Turkish invasion in 1683. Once more rebuilt, the castle was inherited in 1741 by the Doblhoff family in whose possession it remained until the 1960s, when the town of Baden acquired it. In 1971 it became private

133

property again and has since been expanded and converted into a hotel. The building consists of two parts: the original castle and an addition. The old castle has a big square tower through which one enters into a lovely Renaissance courtyard which is now covered and is a very large hall. The formal dining room is also in the old castle. It extends onto a large Renaissance terrace whose Mediterranean appearance reminds one of Italian castles. The terrace overlooks one of the largest rose gardens in Europe and is undoubtedly the most beautiful part of the hotel. The new section of the hotel consists of guest rooms, most of which face the park. There are a total of 103 bedrooms and nine suites, all outfitted with comfortable, traditional furniture and modern bathrooms. There are outdoor tennis courts in the park; indoor tennis courts and a swimming pool, in an adjacent building.

A great asset to the hotel is the Doblhoff Park, which almost completely surrounds it. It is large, has gigantic centuries-old trees, meandering gravel paths, and several ponds with ducks and swans. A trout stream rushes by the castle on its way to the park.

The four-star hotel is open all year. Double rooms with half board cost 2,150 - 2,810 ATS in summer and slightly less at other times.

Excursions:

- There is much to be seen in Baden itself. On the public beach by the Schwechat River is an outdoor thermal pool whose temperature may reach 33°C (91°F). The main spa building with thermal indoor and outdoor swimming pools is popular in all seasons as are the recently renovated elegant gambling casino and the large Kurpark.
- Bus and tram rides to Vienna take 35 - 45 minutes. The bus line ends at the Opernplatz in the very center of Vienna, and the tram line at the nearby Karlsplatz.
- A day trip to Eisenstadt, Rust, and the Neusiedler See takes one into the Pannonian Plain whose flat landscape resembles that of the neighboring Hungary. Both towns have been mentioned in the chapter on Burgenland, the province where they are located. The best way from Baden to Eisenstadt is Route 210 to Ebreichsdorf where you turn right onto Route 16, and then at Müllendorf turn left onto Route 59. This will bring you into the center of Eisenstadt. To get to Rust, continue from Eisenstadt on Route 52. Eisenstadt is about 40 km from Baden and Rust about 20 km more.

HOTEL BURG KRANICHBERG
A-2640 Gloggnitz
Kranichberg 1
Telephone: 02662/8242
Fax: 02662/8386

This castle hotel is about 7 km southeast of Gloggnitz and about 85 km south of Vienna. From Vienna, take the A-2 autobahn to its intersection with Route 56 and follow the latter to Gloggnitz. In Gloggnitz, turn left onto the secondary road toward Kirchberg and St. Corona, which brings you to Burg Kranichberg.

A castle allegedly stood here in Charlemagne's time, but the present one was built by Hermann von Kranichberg, who lived from 1190 to 1255. It was later owned by a succession of very prominent families, and after suffering heavy damage from fire in 1745 was rebuilt by Count Lamberg. In 1769 it was acquired by the Archbisphoric of Vienna and served as summer residence of the Archbishops until 1955. When Dr. Johannes Hübner purchased the castle in 1978, it was severely dilapidated, but since then has been painstakingly restored. The impressive old castle unfortunately is not open to the public, but an adjacent large old farm building has been turned into a hotel. It has 46 rooms and two suites. Some are furnished in the modern style while the furniture in others, although new, looks rustic. The bathrooms are new and well-appointed. The entrance hall and all corridors are spacious and are decorated with suits of armor, old arms, and 18th and 19th century prints. There are conference rooms, a nice restaurant, and a beautiful, large indoor swimming pool with spectacular views through the glass walls of the pool area.

The hotel has a four-star rating and is open all year. Double rooms with half board cost 2,440 ATS. Major credit cards are accepted.
Excursions:
See Schloß Weikersdorf and Burg Bernstein (Burgenland).

HOTEL SCHLOSS KRUMBACH
A-2851 Krumbach
Schloß 1
Telephone: 2647/2209-0
Fax: 2647/2209-88

The village of Krumbach is 80 km south of Vienna and only 8 km from the A-2 autobahn. The castle is in a peaceful country setting on a wooded hill, high above a brook.

It was built by the von Krumbach family in the first half of the 13th century. After the extinction of the Krumbach male line in 1394, it was inherited by the powerful Counts Puchheim, who in the 15th and 16th centuries expanded the castle, added 8 more towers, and turned it into a mighty fortress. Toward the middle of the 17th century, the property was inherited by the Counts and later Princes Pálffy von Erdöd, who owned it until 1875. The castle has since changed hands several times and is now owned by the Meta-Hotels. It became a hotel in 1993. The castle is at the end of a long, climbing drive and is entered through a series of fortified gates. It is a massive, square fortress with rather obvious recent alterations on one side. Everything in the hotel is in perfect order, very new and modern. There are 63 large bedrooms and 4 huge suites with comfortable contemporary furniture and all the latest amenities. There is a very nice indoor swimming pool and a well-equipped conference center. The attractive restaurant is decorated in the traditional style and offers views of the lovely countryside.

The hotel has a five-star rating and is open all year. The price of double rooms with half board is 2,740 ATS. All major credit cards are accepted.

Excursions:

See under Schloß Weikersdorf and Burg Bernstein (Burgenland).

WIEN
(Vienna)

Heroes' Square

Vienna has throughout its long history been the capital of Austria and at the same time also the capital of the province of Lower Austria by which it is completely enclosed. Recently granted the status of a separate province, it is now the ninth and by far the smallest (404 sq. km.) province of Austria. It is without doubt one of the most beautiful capitals in the world, but its size of about 1,600,000 inhabitants makes it disproportionately large for present day Austria.

It was built on a grand scale because it was intended to be the glittering capital of a vast and rich empire. Despite the dismemberment of that empire at the end of World War I, Vienna retains much of its old charm, elegance, and joi de vivre, and continues to be the cultural and economic center of the lands of the former empire.

The relevant part of its history begins in 1156, when Duke Heinrich II von Babenberg made it capital of his state. The city was for many centuries encircled by a huge wall, which twice saved it from the Turks, but also restricted its growth. The wall was demolished in the middle of the 19th century and replaced by the semi-circular Ringstraße, a

139

4 km long, wide, leafy boulevard lined with stately public buildings, among them the Imperial Palace, the Parliament, the City Hall, the University, several museums, the Opera, and a theater. The river that flows through the city is the small and uninspiring Wien rather than the Danube, which runs north of the Inner City. Contrary to the impression created by the name of the Blue Danube Waltz, the Danube is not blue at all but disappointingly muddy. Nevertheless, it is said to look blue to all who are madly in love.

The best starting point for a brief tour of the city is the Opernplatz (Opera Square), where the Ringstraße intersects with Kärntner Straße. The *Staatsoper* (Opera) was built in the Renaissance style and was completed in 1869. Its design drew so much criticism from many quarters (including the Emperor) that one of its two architects committed suicide while the other died of stroke a few months later. The building was completely destroyed by bombs in World War II but was rebuilt in 1955 and now again houses one of the best opera companies in the world. A walk down Kärntner Straße, past the most prestigious and most expensive stores in Austria, takes one to the center of the Inner City and the Stephanstdom (St. Stephen's Cathedral), the principal landmark of Vienna. It is the finest Gothic monument in Austria and one of the most beautiful cathedrals in Europe. Originally built in the 12th century as a Romanesque basilica it was destroyed by fire in the 13th century and rebuilt in the Gothic style at the beginning of the 14th century. It was severely damaged by bombs in World War II but has since been restored. The principal features of its exterior are a 137 m high, slender Gothic spire and a very steeply pitched roof covered with brightly colored glazed tiles arranged in lively patterns. The cathedral is entered through an ornamented Romanesque doorway (1230) from where the Babenbergs dispensed justice. The interior of the cathedral is awe-inspiring and full of priceless treasures. The two most important pieces of art are the Gothic pulpit delicately carved from stone and a beautifully carved, painted and gilded wood altar piece from the 15th century.

At the west corner of the Stephansplatz (Cathedral Square) begins a wide street, the Graben (ditch), which up to the 13th century had indeed been a ditch that marked the southwest boundary of the city. It is now part of Vienna's most chic shopping area. In the Graben stands the 21 m high Trinity Column erected in the 17th century in gratitude for the deliverance of the city from the plague. At the far end of the Graben, turn left into Kohlmarkt Street and at number 14 you will find Demel, the most famous pastry shop in Vienna. Founded more than 200 years ago, it still proudly carries the title of Confectionery to the Imperial Court and offers an unparalleled array of pasteries and cakes. One of the best is the Dobostorte, a chocolate layered cake topped with a layer of crisp caramel. Demel's exquisit hot chocolate and coffee taste particularly good *mit Schlag* (with whipped cream). Kohlmarkt ends at the Hofburg, the Imperial Palace. This is a vast complex begun in the 13th and completed in the 20th century. It has more than 4000 rooms, and numerous courtyards and wings. It is truly a city within a city. It is now the official residence of the Federal Chancellor and also houses several museums, the National Library, and the Spanish Riding School. One could spend days exploring the Palace, but one should at least visit the *Schatzkammer* (Imperial Treasury) in which are displayed treasures collected over a period of about 1000 years. Among them are Charlemagne's sword from the 9th century, the Crown of the Holy Roman Empire from the year 962, the emperor's Holy Lance, at one time thought to be the one with which Christ's chest was pierced, a bowl once believed to be the Holy Grail, an emerald more than 200 carats large, and innumerable other treasures from times long past. Neue Hofburg is the large south wing of the palace completed in 1913 in the Neobaroque style. In front of it is the huge Helden Platz (Heroes' Square) with big equestrian statues of Austria's two most celebrated military leaders, Prince Eugene and Archduke Charles, facing each other from opposite ends of the square. On the other side of the Ring directly across from the square are the imposing buildings of the Museum of Fine Arts and the Natural History Museum separated by a park. In the park is a 20 m high statue of Empress Maria Theresia, surrounded by her generals and advisors, and by Gluck, Mozart, and Haydn, the most prominent composers of her reign. The world famous collection of paintings in the Museum of Fine Arts fills 15 rooms and 24 galleries and takes days to view. Its most outstanding paintings, however, can be seen in much less time by concentrating on Room VIII (Early Dutch paintings) and Room X (1/3 of all existing paintings by Pieter Brueghel the Elder). Room XV is devoted to the 17th and 18th century Dutch painters including Rembrandt and Ruisdael. Dürer's works are displayed in Gallery 15, Holbein's in Gallery 18, and Rembrandt's self portraits in Gallery 23.

Farther up the Ring are the Parliament, in the style of ancient Greek temples, and the Neogothic Rathaus (Town Hall) with a 98 m high tower. Across the street is the Renaissance style Burgtheater and still farther up the Ring on the left, the massive University building that takes a whole city block. The building was erected in the 19th century, but the University itself goes back to 1365.

Despite their joviality, the Viennese have an almost morbid preoccupation with death and the hereafter, and proper burial is to them a matter of paramount importance. They are particularly impressed by the pomp that accompanies burials of the Habsburgs, who have since 1633 been laid to rest in sarcophagi inside the Kaisergruft (Imperial Burial Vault) in the Capuchin Monastery in the Inner City. Many Austrians visit it every day, and thousands upon thousands lined the streets of the Inner City in 1989 for the burial of Zita, the last Empress. In accordance with tradition, the body was brought from St. Stephen's Cathedral to the monastery. A knock on the monastery gate, symbolising the gate of heaven, was answered by the Abbot, impersonating St. Peter. He asked for the name of the person seeking admission. The Empress was introduced as Her Majesty The Empress of Austria, Apostolic Queen of Hungary, and on, and on, and on, until all of her numerous titles had been recited. "St. Peter" responded that he did not know who that was. This interchange in Latin was then repeated with the same outcome. But on the third time around, when the Empress was introduced as Zita, a mere mortal woman with more sins than there are stars in the heaven who was humbly begging to be admitted, the gate opened wide and the voice invited her in to rest forever in peace. The purpose of this touching ceremony enacted at the death of each Emperor was to instill humility into his successor by reminding him that in the eyes of God he was but a common mortal.

Well outside the Inner City is the Schönbrunn (beautiful spring) Palace named after a spring discovered on this spot by an emperor during a hunt in the 16th century. The hunting lodge originally built there is now within the city limits and has grown into a 200 m long, 1,441 room, summer residence of the Habsburgs. The palace was designed by Fischer von Erlach the Elder in the Baroque style and was built at the end of the 17th century. About 40 resplendent Baroque rooms are open to the public as is also Emperor Franz Josef's Spartan bedroom with a standard military bed. In the 2 sq. km large formal gardens are fountains, statues, a botanical garden, and a small zoo established in 1552. This zoo is thought to be the oldest in Europe.

Of all the magnificent buildings in Vienna none was built in better taste and more pleasing proportions than the Belvedere Palace. It is just south of the Ring, immediately behind Schwarzenbergplatz and the Hotel im Palais Schwarzenberg. The palace actually consists of two buildings, the older Lower and the newer Upper Belvedere. Both were designed by the famous Baroque architect Johann Lukas von Hildebrandt and were built in the early part of the 18th century for Prince Eugene of Savoy. He resided in the Lower Belvedere and used the Upper for receptions and other festive occasions. The Palace grounds are entered from the south, through a huge and lavishly decorated wrought iron gate, which opens onto the park and a large round pool in front of the formal entrance to the Upper Palace. This stately aristocratic abode is a masterpiece of Baroque elegance and refinement, and despite its great opulence is completely devoid of base showiness and banal ostentation.

Information on Vienna can be obtained at Tourist Information, A-1 Vienna, Kärntner Straße 38, Telephone: 0222/5138892.

Vienna

SCHLOSS WILHELMINENBERG
A-1160 Wien
Savoyenstraße 2
Telephone: 0222/458503-0
Fax: 0222/454876

The hotel is situated in its own park on a hill on the western outskirts of Vienna, 15-20 minutes by car from the Opernplatz. Its history begins in 1781 when Field-Marshal Count von Lascy built here a small castle which only three years later, in 1784, was bought by the Russian ambassador, Prince Galitzin. The castle with the woods and fields around it was inherited by Count Rumjanzow in 1795, and in 1824 was bought by Prince Montléart who in 1838 enlarged the castle by adding two wings. When his son died in 1887, the property was inherited by the son's wife, Princess Wilhelmine, a philanthropist after whom the hill on which the castle stands was renamed. After her death in 1895, the property was acquired by a Habsburg archduke who in 1908 had the castle further expanded and redesigned into a rather pretentious palace. After the fall of the Empire, the castle became an orphanage, then a school, and in 1988, a hotel.

The hotel is a very large white edifice with a high central section and two symmetrical wings. The entrance hall is enormous; next to it is a large dining room. The hotel features 91 bedrooms, all with bathrooms, and most also with pretty views. The rooms are comfortably but frugally outfitted with contemporary furniture lacking any distinct style.

A grand building like this, in a beautiful and peaceful setting within a short distance from the center of Vienna, begs to be upgraded to a first class hotel.

It is now a three-star hotel open all year. Double rooms with breakfast cost 615 - 730 ATS, and half board an additional 210 ATS per person. Major credit cards are accepted.

HOTEL IM PALAIS
SCHWARZENBERG
A-1030 Wien
Schwarzenbergplatz 9
Telephone: 0222/784515
Fax: 0222/784714

This is certainly not an ordinary hotel, nor even an outstanding one, but one that falls into a category all by itself. Strictly speaking, it is not even a castle but a palace whose purpose from its inception was to display the immense power and wealth of the princely family that owned it, to enhance that family's social status, and to provide the family a life of elegance and luxury. Lukas von Hildebrandt, one of the two greatest Austrian Baroque architects,designed the palace and its formal gardens for a prince who died before the palace could be completed. Prince Schwarzenberg then acquired the property and engaged the services of the other great master of Baroque architecture, Fischer von Erlach the Elder, who unfortunately did not live to see the project through. His work was continued by his almost equally famous son, Josef Emmanuel, and was finally completed in 1732. The palace is in an 18 acre park with an impressive fountain, beautiful lawns, trees, statues, and gravel paths. It borders on the Belvedere Palace park described earlier in this chapter.. Like the Belvedere, the Schwarzenberg Palace also is a well-proportioned Baroque edifice whose elegant lines are in perfect harmony with its surroundings. It is a fine legacy of the 18th century, a time when sophistication in art, music, language, manners, and attire reached its peak. The palace sustained considerable damage at the end of World War II but has since been restored by the present Prince Schwarzenberg, who, when in Vienna, resides here. A part of the palace is now a historic landmark hotel in the heart of the city, a throwback to a more leisurely era of great elegance, gracious service, and refined luxury.

The hotel has 38 rooms and suites, beautifully decorated with antiques and tastefully furnished in the traditional style. Bedrooms facing the park behind the hotel are especially desirable. The entrance hall is fairly small and unpretentious, but there are several very formal halls used on special occasions. The most ornate among them and almost museum-like in splendor and perfection are the domed formal Entrance Hall and the Marble Hall, whose walls and ceilings are covered with ornamental plaster moldings and 18th century paintings. Equally beautiful is the Rubens Hall on whose walls hang two large paintings by Rubens. Dining rooms vary in size and style but not in elegance. The restaurant on the enclosed terrace facing the park is particularly attractive and is favored by the Viennese high society. The cuisine, the presentation of food, the service, and the ambiance are among the best in Vienna.

This truly unique hotel has been awarded the highest rating, which it certainly deserves. It is open all year and all major credit cards are honored. Double rooms cost 3,800 - 5,300 ATS and suites 5,300 - 7,300 ATS. Breakfast is not included in the room price and costs an additional 170 ATS a person for a continental and 270 ATS for a buffet breakfast. As the hotel is only 15 minutes on foot from the center of Vienna, you also can breakfast at one of a number of charming in-town coffee shops for which Vienna is famous.

For elegant dining outside the hotel try the *Korso* restaurant at the nearby Hotel Bristol at Mahlerstraße 2 across the street from the Opera, or the *Steirer Eck,* Rasumofskygasse 2, which many consider the best restaurant in Vienna though not necessarily the most elegant one. Both restaurants are outstanding and very expensive.

One can dine very well at a cozy and folksy *Heuriger* inn for a

Vienna

small fraction of the price at these restaurants. *Heurigen* are charming taverns in the suburbs of Grinzing, Sievering, Nußdorf, and others. They offer copious amounts of delicious, typically Austrian fare in a very informal and congenial setting. The food is accompanied by local wine of recent vintage (*Heuriger* means this year's) and also often by Viennese music played by small music bands. Some of these taverns, however, regularly attract bus loads of tourists. It is, therefore, best to seek advice from the hotel concierge as to which of the many *Heurigen* to choose.